Researching into Learning Resources

In Colleges and Universities

**CHRIS HIGGINS, JUDY READING
& PAUL TAYLOR**

**KOGAN
PAGE**

The Practical Research Series
Series Editor: Kate Ashcroft

Researching into Teaching Methods in Colleges and Universities,
  Clinton Bennett, Lorraine Foreman-Peck and Chris Higgins
Researching into Assessment and Evaluation in Colleges and Universities,
  Kate Ashcroft and David Palacio
Researching into Equal Opportunities in Colleges and Universities,
  Kate Ashcroft, Stephen Bigger and David Coates
Researching into Learning Resources in Colleges and Universities,
  Chris Higgins, Judy Reading and Paul Taylor

First published in 1996

Kogan Page Limited
120 Pentonville Road
London N1 9JN

British Library Cataloguing in Publication Data

A CIP record for this book is available from the British Library.

ISBN 0 7494 1771 4

Typeset by Kogan Page
Printed and bound in Great Britain by Biddles Ltd, Guildford and King's Lynn

Contents

Chapter 1

Series Introduction

Kate Ashcroft

The research that colleges and universities engage in covers a very wide spectrum, including basic research into fundamental problems as well as entrepreneurial work, often contracted by a particular customer. Each of the books in this series is focused on a particular form of research: that of small-scale insider research. Each looks at issues of teaching, learning and management within colleges and universities from the point of view of the novice researcher. The aim is to provide you with starting points for research that will help you understand and improve your practice, that of your students and the context for learning and teaching that your institution provides. The research that you undertake may also help you to understand the context in which teaching and learning is managed and should provide you with the raw material for publication in research-based media.

The series is aimed at creating a range of quick and easy to read handbooks, so you can get started on research into aspects of your teaching and students' learning. Each book includes a version of this introductory chapter by the series editor about insider research, its principles and methods. If you have read the series introduction in another of the books in the series, you may wish to skip parts of this chapter and go straight to the section, *Main issues and topics covered in this book* towards the end of this chapter.

Each book in the series also includes a concluding chapter by the series editor that provides guidelines on writing for publication and information about publishing outlets, including an annotated list of publishers and journals interested in educational research in further and higher education in general and, in particular, learning resources.

The chapters in this book are focused on contemporary issues relating to resources for learning. They include a range of examples of research instruments and suggestions as to how you might use or adapt

1

them to your own context for enquiry. The starting points for research cover the following areas:

- the perspectives of the main participants in the use of learning resources;
- the context in which they operate;
- their existing practice;
- their existing values; and
- the relationships between the context and the values and practice.

A range of methods used in insider research into learning and learning resources is included within the research tasks.

None of the books includes sufficient information for you to complete a research project for publication. You will need to find out more about the particular aspects of learning resources and the research methodology that you decide to use. Similarly, the book will introduce you to some of the theoretical frameworks open to you, but the discussion will not be deep enough, of itself, to ensure that your research is 'grounded in theory'. For these reasons, an annotated reading list is included at the end of each chapter.

Synopsis of the Series

This book is one of a series that includes the following books:

- *Researching into Assessment and Evaluation in Colleges and Universities* (Ashcroft and Palacio, 1996);
- *Researching into Teaching Methods in Colleges and Universities* (Bennett, Foreman-Peck and Higgins, 1996);
- *Researching into Student Learning and Support in Colleges and Universities* (Jones, Siraj-Blatchford and Ashcroft, forthcoming);
- *Researching into Learning Resources in Colleges and Universities* (Higgins, Reading and Taylor, 1996); and
- *Researching into Equal Opportunities in Colleges and Universities* (Ashcroft, Bigger and Coates, 1996).

The series is designed to appeal to lecturers in further and higher education who are interested in developing research skills and who would find concrete suggestions for research and some exemplar research questions and instruments helpful. For this reason, we have aimed for an accessible and readable style of writing. Care has been taken to keep sentences and paragraphs short and the writing practical, informal and personal. We have tried to avoid using technical terms and jargon unnecessarily, but where these have to be included, we have tried to explain them in as simple a way as possible.

Increasingly, lecturers are required to produce regular research papers. In the UK, the process of research rating means that lecturers in universities restrict their career opportunities if they do not engage regularly in research and publication. (I describe the process of research rating in the introductory chapter to Bennett *et al.*, 1996.) Many do not know where to start. Others are unable to manage their time in order to incorporate their research and publication alongside their teaching work. Some feel that a commitment to research would detract from their preferred role as teachers.

The series aims to provide you with a framework of ideas and starting points for research which can be carried out alongside your current practice. The books present these ideas in such a way that, rather than detracting from your practice, they might enhance it. They introduce methods for you to use (adapted or unadapted) for researching into your own teaching. For example, in Chapter 4 the process of discourse analysis is described. This process is applicable to a variety of research problems. Most of the ideas do not require visits outside of your institution and suggest data that could be available with a fairly modest outlay of energy.

You should find the books useful if you are new to teaching and/or if you are an experienced lecturer who needs or wishes to develop a research and publication profile within education. In the case of higher education, this is a major focus that involves all tutors. You may be under pressure to publish for the first time in order to contribute to research rating exercises. You might be undertaking a qualification that includes a research element. A masters degree or doctorate is an increasing requirement for promotion in further and higher education. In the UK, more masters degree courses are being developed and geared towards this sector. In higher education, many staff are now expected to achieve a doctorate. Some of the starting points within this book could be developed into a fairly sophisticated research project.

You may be interested in researching your own practice for its own sake. For instance, you may wish to explore your students' needs in relation to the learning resources available. The interest in insider research is percolating into colleges and universities from the action research movement within schools and may grow at a comparable rate.

Insider Research and the Model of Reflection

Insider research is a form of participant research. It is principally about understanding and improving practice within the researcher's institution. It can be focused on a problem and involve cycles of data collection, evaluation and reflection, as in action research. Other books in the series that take you step by step through the process of action research are Ashcroft and Palacio (1996) and Bennett *et al.* (1996).

Insider research need not be problem-centred. It is an appropriate approach for a matter of personal curiosity or interest that you decide to investigate in a systematic way. Many tutors who have used the approach have found that insider research is an empowering process. It often comes up with surprises and enables you to see problems in new ways. It is probably the most effective way of exploring the functioning of real-life classrooms and investigating the effects of your interventions. It deals with the real problems and issues you face and, in doing so, may transform those problems and the way you construe teaching and learning. It has a moral base, in that it allows you to explore your actions and those of others in the light of the values that supposedly underpin them. The consideration of your own values and their relation to accepted notions of ethical research are important matters in insider research.

The series is built on the model of the reflective practitioner of education as described by Dewey (1916) and developed by Zeichner, Ashcroft and others (see, for instance, Ashcroft, 1987; Ashcroft and Griffiths, 1989; Deakin, 1982; Isaac and Ashcroft, 1986; Stenhouse, 1979; Zeichner, 1982 and Zeichner and Teitlebaum, 1982). The model takes the view that 'knowledge' is not absolute or static and that lecturers in further and higher education should take an active role in constructing and reconstructing it. This suggests that educationists have some sort of moral responsibility for the truth, and indeed that it is part of their duty to act as whistle-blowers when the powerful define truth in ways convenient for their purposes. It sees reflective practice as much more than a passive 'thinking about'. It embraces active professional development, directed at particular qualities: open-mindedness, commitment and responsibility. The enquiry considers the question of 'What works?' but also moves on to pose questions of worthwhileness. This demands investigation into action, intervention and the perspectives of a number of the participants in the educational process: students, tutors, institutional managers, employers, funders and community representatives. It also suggests that intentions, attitudes and values are explored, as well as behaviour and outcomes.

Each of the qualities of open-mindedness, commitment and responsibility has particular definitions and demands prerequisite skills and understandings. This series of books is partially directed at helping you to acquire research skills and skills of analysis. For instance, open-mindedness requires that you seek out and analyse the perspectives of each of the stakeholders in education. For this reason, this book includes a variety of examples of ways to collect and organize data that you might use to find out about the behaviours, thoughts, attitudes and experience of students, other lecturers, managers, employers and others. Our intention in introducing you to various research processes is to enable you to collect data and to analyse them in the light of your emerging theory of practice (see Argyris and Schon, 1974, for more details of this notion of theory in action).

Commitment implies a real and sustained attachment to the value of your work and to improving its context. You need optimism to sustain this: to believe that you are one of the stakeholders in the institution and community, and that you have the duty and power to effect changes and to secure the appropriate teaching and learning environment for your students. This is not easy, particularly in circumstances where resources are very short or where you work within an autocratic or chaotic management regime. Insider research cannot solve these kinds of problems, but it may help you to understand their nature and go some way to helping you to see how limited time might be used more effectively and how the stress caused by time pressures can be reduced.

Responsibility implies that you are interested in the long- and short-term consequences of action. This means that you collect evidence as to your effectiveness and the intended and unintended outcomes of your teaching and management. We suggest a range of research instruments that may help you to discover what you actually do (as opposed to what you think you do) in the course of your work, what effects your behaviour has on others, how they see it and the attitudes resulting from it.

In slightly more positive circumstances, insider research can be empowering. It is one way of finding out about the needs and interests of others and expressing these in terms that create a powerful case for change. For this reason, we have included a range of starting points for research that will enable you to enquire into management issues and the working of your institution.

We have stated that research skills are an essential prerequisite to reflective practice. This should not be taken to mean that they are sufficient. Reflective practice in teaching also requires that you acquire a range of other skills. These include technical teaching skills, such as voice projection; interpersonal skills such as counselling skills and the ability to work as part of a team; communication skills in a variety of contexts; and the ability to criticize the status quo from a moral point of view. Insider research, perhaps uniquely, can help you to acquire each of these skills. By providing feedback on your actions, insider research directs you to problems that you are creating or failing to solve. You can then experiment with new ways of approaching them and use insider research to provide information on the effectiveness of your new ways of thinking and acting. We suggest a range of evaluation methods that you may want to use to explore your practice and that of others.

Reflective practice is an ideal that can be its most painful when it is achieved. It requires that you question your deepest beliefs and compare your actions with your values. In doing this, you may find that you must abandon cherished beliefs or practices. Despite the loss that change brings and the risks that it involves, the value of reflective practice is in the process of continual questioning and renewal that is essential for professional development and growth in understanding. Nobody is able to sustain reflective practice at all times. During the process of teaching and research you will sometimes delude yourself. You may frame your problem according to assumptions that you feel comfortable with, you may interpret data to fit your preferred solution, or you may fail to notice the most important data. For this reason, we suggest that your methods and interpretation should be made public in some way. You need other people to challenge your assumptions and to help you explore the ethical issues that always underlie research.

Research in Colleges and Universities

An increasing number of people expect to be educated, at least to degree level. For instance, in the UK, the proportion of young people going into higher education has doubled in recent years. When the members of this educated population enter colleges and universities, they expect to be taught by people who are expert at a very high level. This expertise is generally achieved through research and publication or through higher degree work that involves research. Education at this level is being seen as an increasingly rigorous process. Quality and standards in the sector have come under continuous scrutiny. One of the determinants in the assessment of quality is the level of expertise of staff. Staff who aspire to promotion may have to obtain higher level qualifications that include substantial research (Ashcroft and Foreman-Peck, 1995).

The growth of the pool of highly educated people means that there is increasing competition for permanent posts in colleges and universities. These posts usually go to those who can provide evidence that they are more 'expert' than their competitors. In the UK the number of staff on fixed-term contracts in universities and colleges is growing. In the USA, a glut of highly educated professors means that the proportion of part-time staff in colleges and universities has doubled in the last 20 years (Irwin, 1995). The emphasis in universities on research ratings and the decision in many Western countries to make these public has created a 'publish or die' culture. University lecturers are expected to publish papers and books with increasing regularity. Where colleges aspire to include higher level courses within their portfolio, they often find that the staff who teach such courses are expected to demonstrate a research record that equals that of colleagues in the university sector.

Busy lecturers need to find a time-efficient way to research and publish. If you engage in insider research, you are likely to find your results are interesting and that they might have more general application. A number of my colleagues who engage in fairly small-scale research of this type, mainly for their own interest, have then published the resulting papers in refereed journals.

In effect, I am suggesting 'quick and dirty' research as appropriate for the hard-working lecturer who wants to improve his or her practice. This can be somewhat refined and elaborated for publication. There is interest from editors and readers of journals in small-scale, modest research that focuses on the real dilemmas that lecturers face.

On the other hand, insider research does have its weaknesses. In particular it is prone to self-justification and can be very inward looking. If you are to be a successful insider researcher, you will need to identify a *critical* group or community that will help you identify appropriate research questions, refine your research instruments, evaluate your reflections and data as you go along and help to ensure that you are considering ethical issues. You will also need to seek alternative interpretations of your data from a number of sources and to read widely, in order to locate your insights in a wider context.

When I have engaged in this kind of research and publication, the key thing I have discovered is the need to relate my findings to a theoretical framework (see, for instance, Ashcroft and Griffiths, 1990 or Ashcroft and Peacock, 1993). Very occasionally, I have developed my own framework, but more usually I have used an existing one to analyse my findings. Without such analysis, the results of insider research tend to be anecdotal and descriptive. Such work may be publishable, but in magazines and newspapers, rather than research journals.

Starting Points for Research: Values and Practice

We do not provide a total blueprint for research. This would be impossible, given the variety of contexts in which the readers of the series work and the variety of findings they are likely to come up with. Even if it were possible to lay out a complete research project for you to follow, we would not wish to do so. A large part of the new knowledge and understanding gained from research comes from the stimulus to creativity that asking your own questions and looking at preliminary data provide. In collecting your own data and then asking questions of yourself such as 'What do I need to know to interpret these data?', 'How can I get at the meanings behind these data?' or, 'What other data do I need?', you will come up with transformational resolutions to research questions that are far more innovative and creative than any the authors could suggest. Therefore, you should feel free to interpret research tasks widely: to adapt and alter suggested foci for research and ideas for data collection to fit your own context and, most importantly, to go beyond the first cycle of data collection to ask your own questions.

It is important to be aware of the limitations of small-scale research. If you claim a spurious objectivity to your work, you are likely to miss the most important strength of small-scale research: the opportunity it offers to you to explore your existing practice and that of others, the stated values that underpin this practice and the relationship between those values and the practice. Practice may seem to you to be the most objective of these elements but, in exploring practice, it is important to realize that it is often more difficult to get at it than first appears. There is often a gap between what people (including you) say and believe that they do and what they actually do. Thus, self-report may not capture the data you need. Other methods are mediated by the values of the person undertaking the analysis. For instance, if you want to investigate the effectiveness of computer-assisted learning, the results you get may depend upon the methods you use, the questions you ask and the categories you choose in order to organize any data you collect.

Each of us has values that we espouse. Many teachers can articulate them in relation to certain criteria. For example, most of us believe in encouraging students to become autonomous learners. You may want to dig deeper than this to explore the various ways autonomy may be defined by teachers and how these definitions are or may be incompatible. The series explores the values that are held by each of the stakeholders in education, the implications of these for teaching, learning and management, and the extent to which they are compatible or raise dilemmas that must be resolved. For example, institutional managers may favour forms of teaching based on independent learning, but such methods may suit particular types of students better than others.

Research Issues Covered in the Books

The research issues and perspectives that are researched in this series are set out in more detail in Ashcroft and Palacio (1996). I summarize these below.

The series covers the investigation of a variety of perspectives. Each of the stakeholders in education has its own priorities and the people working within them have their own satisfactions and frustrations. The quality of the services that an institution provides in support of student learning are in part determined by these perspectives. For example, you might be interested in exploring the perspectives of students on various library services.

A range of research issues are suggested within each book in the series. These include:

- values and practice: the perceptions of each of the stakeholders in education on various aspects of the educative process;
- attitudes: how they influence how stakeholders see and judge reality;
- motivation and learning;
- behaviour: the gap and the link between beliefs and learning and actual behaviour;
- educational priorities: the priorities of each of the stakeholders in education, and the extent to which they are compatible;
- efficiency and effectiveness: how each affects aspects of the students' learning experience;
- criteria for judgements: including definitions of the problems education faces;
- objectives, processes or outcomes;
- relationships between people: how each party to and group concerned with education is affected by the others;
- justice, equality and the ways that diversity is catered for within education: consideration of conflicting interests with education;

- ethics and control issues in learning: how they are construed by the various parties, the way that good practice might be defined, and the way that interests compete and are resolved.

The Quantitative and Qualitative Research Traditions in Education

Research in education may fall into the quantitative tradition and focus on the collection (usually of large numbers) of numerical data, or into the qualitative tradition and look in depth at a smaller number of instances. It may be focused on discovery or on the improvement of practice.

There is much ideological baggage that now surrounds the qualitative and quantitative traditions in education. You need to get to grips with this debate so that you understand the strengths and weaknesses of each. Within education there has been a shift from respect for models of research based on the scientific tradition of experimental and quasi-experimental research methods, towards qualitative, descriptive methods within naturalistic settings, first pioneered in subjects such as anthropology and now termed 'ethnographic' methods. Each of these models has its strength and weakness. The qualitative tradition is criticized because of its limited scope, particularity and 'subjectivity', the quantitative tradition because of the triviality of its findings, their lack of application to the real life 'messiness' of classrooms and because most practitioners of such research were expert in research and not in education, and therefore addressed other researchers, rather than teachers.

Quantitative research must be judged on its own terms. For instance, questions of usefulness or applicability may not be the point. Quantitative research is 'good' research if the results are valid and reliable. Reliability (to what extent the context and results can be replicated) is sometimes over-emphasized at the expense of other aspects of validity, such as the assumptions underpinning the questions asked and categories used.

Research in the qualitative tradition must also be judged by appropriate criteria. It should not be criticized for 'subjectivity', unless it claims to be objective. Such research is often problem-centred and pragmatic, and so the notion of proof becomes irrelevant. The validity of the research depends on the extent to which the situation, actions, causes and effects are described convincingly. The quality of the research may depend on interjudgemental reliability (whether the readers, researchers and the actors in the research situation describe and interpret the findings in the same way). 'Subjective' factors are taken into account in judging its quality: at a pragmatic level (whether the problem was solved to the satisfaction of all the parties involved); and at a moral level (the moral basis of actions by the researcher is often open to scrutiny – did they ask the right question, were they 'up front' about their thoughts, feelings and motives, were the values that underpinned the research made explicit?)

Quantitative research methods in education make claims to reliability because of some kind of objectivity or because the test used has been found to work similarly in other situations (for instance, by other researchers, against other tests, and so on). External validity (the extent to which the results of a study can be generalized to other times and places) is usually a matter of the situation and population studied: the size of sample, its 'typicality' and the categories used. Campbell and Stanley (1963) give one of the best outlines of factors that commonly jeopardize the validity of such research. The researcher may present him or herself as a detached outsider observing a situation or seeking to disprove a hypothesis. Thus, some attempt may be made to control the variables in the situation and many instances of a particular result may be described before it can be considered significant. Statistical significance is determined by a standard statistical test.

The kind of insider research that may be most appropriate to reflective practice occasionally uses experimental methods and 'soft' quantitative techniques, but relies more heavily on the qualitative research tradition. It makes few claims for reliability and external validity. Instead, it seeks to describe a particular situation in all its complexity. For this reason, the control of variables is usually inappropriate. The reader determines whether the results are, or are not, relevant. So that the reader can answer the question, 'Might this research have some significance to me in my particular situation?', they must know the author's claims to expert knowledge, the extent to which his or her conclusions and interpretation of the situation have been tested against the interpretations of other parties, the assumptions that the researcher made, and his or her emotional responses to issues and those of others. Elliott (1991) provides a good account of the strengths and weaknesses of research within the qualitative research tradition.

Each of the traditions makes its own assumptions about cause and effect. The quantitative tradition presupposes that the truth can be separated from the perspective of the observer. The qualitative tradition implies that truth is intimately connected to the thoughts, feelings and assumptions of the participants in education. One model tidies and simplifies reality in order to look at and analyse it; in the other, the full messiness of reality is explored. One might caricature the weaknesses of each by saying that the quantitative tradition says something true in the experimental context, that may be untrue, trivial or unimportant in the reality of the classroom, and the qualitative tradition may say something interesting or important about one situation, but there is no way of knowing whether it is the truth. The quantitative tradition tends to be inductive and the qualitative tradition deductive. Perhaps the best research studies will use some aspects of each. What is important is that, whatever methods you use, you take the time to find out about the construction of appropriate research instruments and admit to the threats to the validity and reliability of the findings inherent within the approach you take.

Data Collection Techniques

The authors provide you with starting points only for research. There is a very wide range of research methods and approaches open to you. These are described in some detail within the books in the series as follows:

Ashcroft, K, Bigger, S and Coates, D (1996) *Researching into Equal Opportunities in Colleges and Universities*
Semantic differential tests
Focus group techniques
Attitude tests
Database interrogation
Questionnaires: structured, unstructured and open
Scenario analysis.

Bennett, C, Foreman-Peck, L and Higgins, C (1996) *Researching into Teaching Methods in Colleges and Universities*
Using IT for qualitative data analysis
Emerging data categories
Action research process
Defining a database
Observation: structured and structured.

Jones, M, Siraj-Blatchford, J and Ashcroft, K (1996) *Researching into Student Learning and Support in Colleges and Universities*
Emerging data categories

Symbolic interactionism
Deconstructionism.

Ashcroft, K and Palacio, D (1996) *Researching into Evaluation and
Assessment in Colleges and Universities*
Action research process
Validity and reliability.

Higgins, C, Reading, J and Taylor, P (1996) *Researching into Learning
Resources in Colleges and Universities*
Systems analysis.

The advantages and problems of each of the various methods are
described in the introductory chapters of Bennett *et al.* (1996) and
Ashcroft *et al.* (1996). They may be used separately or in conjunction to
create the fuller picture that is required of a case study.

Most of the research suggested in the series is small-scale and local
and so we do not discuss methods of statistical analysis. It may be that
you become inspired to undertake a more major study, in which case
there are a variety of computer programs that may help you to analyse
your data (see for instance, Bennett *et al.*, 1996 for more detail on the
use of information technology for qualitative data analysis), or you may
find a book such as Cohen and Manion (1985) useful. If you intend to
use statistical analysis, it is important that you make this decision at the
start of the data collection process. The method you use will affect the
form of the data you should collect. You will probably find all sorts of
problems if you collect your data and then look round for a means of
analysing it.

The important thing is never to claim more for your research than is
justified by your methods, the data you have collected and your analysis.
Small-scale research is unlikely to push back the frontiers of knowledge,
but it can sometimes empower the reader, who may be inspired by a
report of research into practice that chimes with their own experience.
It is almost impossible to prove anything in education. You need to be
very tentative in your conclusions. Because it is almost impossible to
isolate variables in real educational situations, it is seldom possible to
say that a particular stimulus *caused* a particular *effect.* Even if you get
apparently clear-cut results, generally the best that can be said is that,
in the circumstances you investigated, it appears that one thing may be
associated with another.

Main Issues and Topics Covered in this Book

Of all the books in the series, this book is the most focused on the process of enquiry as a means of understanding the issues. The research tasks are truly integrated into the book's content. For this reason, you may find that reading a particular research task, even if you do not intend to use it, will help you to exemplify the ideas that are sketched in the intervening text.

Chapter 2 is focused on the resource environment and the ways that it is influenced. The effects of such an environment on curriculum design and the choices that may become possible with regard to methods of course delivery are considered. One such mode, resource-based learning, is looked at in some detail, together with its links to open, distance and flexible learning. Recent developments in the resources available for learning are analysed, especially in relation to the new technologies. Finally, the uses of more traditional learning resources are discussed.

In Chapter 3, the authors consider the institutional context for researching into learning resources, especially in relation to the changing circumstances within which institutions must operate. They explore the ways that institutions, lecturers and students have responded to these and the new emphasis on systems to support learning and to assure its quality. The changing role of support staff as supporters of student learning is looked at in some detail. Finally, the institutional framework for controlling resources and for identifying resources and staff development priorities is considered.

Chapter 4 focuses on the links between resources and teaching. It looks at computer-assisted learning, the developing theoretical frameworks that may underpin its use in education and their links with theories of learning and learning styles and strategies. These notions are contrasted with more traditional teaching methods.

Chapter 5 looks at the student as a principal stakeholder in the education process. The effects of the market metaphor, with the notion of student as customer, are explored and, in particular, the contribution of learning resources to meeting student needs. Patterns of course provision and their resource implications are considered in a climate of severe financial constraints. Strategies for coping with the dilemmas raised by the tensions between student expectation and rights and the resources environment for learning are explored, including the opportunities and costs of more open forms of learning. The particular needs of students with specific learning needs are considered.

Chapter 6 explores the evaluation of the resource environment and the assessment of its effects on student learning. Ways of designing the resource environment to facilitate desired outcomes are considered and linked to specific models of learning. Finally, the authors look at ways of assessing the quality of resource provision, including the application of models of quality management and quality standards.

In the series conclusion, I suggest some ways of increasing your chances of getting published and describe the process of writing. I suggest that it is important to develop a sense of audience for the book or article proposal as well as for the actual product. I include annotated lists of journals and book publishers, describing the kinds of books or articles they are interested in publishing and the lists or issues that they are currently developing.

Annotated Reading List

Andresen, L *et al.* (1993) *Strategies for Assessing Students,* Birmingham: Staff and Educational Development Association.
A guide to managing assessment as part of teaching.
Angelo, T A and Cross, K P (1993) *Classroom Assessment Techniques: A handbook for college teachers,* London: Jossey Bass.
A good source of proformas and ideas for looking at assessment.
Argyris, C and Schon, D (1974) *Theory into Practice,* Beckenham: Croom Helm.
The definitive book on the relationships between the theories that people hold about their teaching and the theories that they develop in action.
Ashworth, A and Harvey, R (1993) *Quality in Further and Higher Education,* Jessica Kingsley.
An account of total quality management, performance indicators, and systems for assessing standards.
Brown, S and Dove, P (eds) (1990) *Self and Peer Assessment,* Birmingham: Staff and Educational Development Association.
A collection of papers discussing theoretical approaches and practical working materials from different disciplines.
Brown, S, Jones, G and Rawnsley, S (eds) (1993) *Observing Teaching,* Birmingham: Staff and Educational Development Association.
This book is concerned with inquiring into practice in colleges and universities. It covers issues in the appraisal of teaching (who should do it, what should be observed and how). The focus is on professional development, rather than research within higher education.
Bell, J (1987) *Doing your Research Project,* Buckingham: Open University Press.
This book deals with research across the disciplines, rather than teaching and learning in further and higher education.

Cohen, L and Manion, L (1985) *Research Methods in Education,* (2nd edn),
Beckenham: Croom Helm.
A comprehensive account of the major research methods in education. It
is not easy to read, and I would argue with its assumption that educational
research should be scientific, but its critique of the approach we adopt
provides a useful counterbalance. The book covers most of the techniques
in educational research, as well as more technical aspects such as grid
analysis and multidimensional measurement.

Gibbs, G (ed.) (1984 and 1985) *Alternatives in Assessment 1,* and *Alternatives in
Assessment 2,* Birmingham: Staff and Educational Development
Association.
Case studies of different methods of assessment found in higher
education only.

Gibbs, G *et al., 53 Interesting Things to do...,* Bristol: TES.
This series is very popular and sells well. The books are about 140–160
pages long and provide some useful pointers for thinking about teaching
and learning. The focus is on practice, rather than research, but this can
give you a starting point for an evaluation or intervention study.

Green, D (1993) *What is Quality in Higher Education?,* Buckingham: Open
University Press.
A report of a national research project on the assessment of quality, in
higher education only.

Hammersley, M and Atkinson, P (1983) *Ethnography Principles in Practice,*
London: Tavistock.
A reasonably accessible account of ethnographic methods and their
relationship to the social world. It includes a critical analysis of case study,
observation, interviewing and ways of filing and recording data.

McKernan, J (1991) *Curriculum Action Research: A handbook of methods and
resources for the reflective practitioner,* London: Kogan Page.
This book is a good introduction to action research. It contains many
useful suggestions for collecting data.

Smith, B and Brown, S (eds) (1994) *Research, Teaching and Learning in Higher
Education,* London: Kogan Page.
A collection of reports of research undertaken by experienced education
developers within higher education.

Thorpe, M (1993) *Evaluating Open and Distance Learning,* Harlow: Longman.
Covers how to evaluate one type of learning programme.

References

Argyris, C and Schon, D (1974) *Theory into Practice,* Beckenham: Croom Helm.
Ashcroft, K. (1987) 'The history of an innovation', *Assessment and Evaluation in
Higher Education,* 12, 1, 37–45.
Ashcroft, K, Bigger, S and Coates, D (1996) *Researching into Equal Opportunities in
Colleges and Universities,* London: Kogan Page.

Ashcroft, K and Foreman-Peck, L (1994) *Managing Teaching and Learning in Further and Higher Education*, London: Falmer Press.

Ashcroft, K and Foreman-Peck, L (1995) *The Lecturer's Guide to Quality and Standards in Colleges and Universities*, London: Falmer Press.

Ashcroft, K and Griffiths, M (1989) 'Reflective teachers and reflective tutors: school experience in an initial teacher education course', *Journal of Education for Teaching*, 15, 1, 35–52.

Ashcroft, K and Griffiths, M (1990) 'Action research in initial teacher education', in Zuber-Skerritt, O (ed.) *Action Research in Higher Education*, Brisbane: Griffith University Press.

Ashcroft, K and Palacio, D (1996) *Researching into Evaluation and Assessment in Colleges and Universities*, London: Kogan Page.

Ashcroft, K and Peacock, E (1993) 'An evaluation of the progress, experience and employability of mature students on the BEd course at Westminster College, Oxford', *Assessment and Evaluation in Higher Education*, 18, 1, 57–70.

Bennett, C, Foreman-Peck, F and Higgins, C (1996) *Researching into Teaching Methods in Colleges and Universities*, London: Kogan Page.

Campbell, D T and Stanley, J C (1963) *Experimental and Quasi-Experimental Designs for Research*, Chicago: Rand McNally.

Cohen, L and Manion, L (1985) *Research Methods in Education* (2nd edn), Beckenham: Croom Helm.

Deakin University (1982) *The Action Research Reader*, Victoria: Deakin University Press.

Dewey, J (1916) *Democracy and Education*, New York: The Free Press.

Elliott, J (1991) *Action Research for Educational Change*, Milton Keynes: Open University.

Higgins, C, Reading, J and Taylor, P (1996) *Researching into Learning Resources in Colleges and Universities*, London: Kogan Page.

Irwin, A (1995) 'Gypsy professors roam US campuses', *The Times Higher Education Supplement*, 24 February.

Isaac, J and Ashcroft, K (1986) 'A leap into the practical', in Nias, J and Groundwater-Smith, S (eds) *The Enquiring Teacher: Supporting and sustaining teacher research*, London: Falmer Press.

Jones, M, Siraj-Blatchford, J and Ashcroft, K (1996) *Researching into Student Learning and Support in Colleges and Universities*, London: Kogan Page.

Stenhouse, L (1979) 'What is action research?', *CARE*, University of East Anglia, Mimeograph.

Zeichner, K and Teitlebaum, K (1982) 'Personalised and inquiry oriented education: an analysis of two approaches to the development of curriculum in field-based experience', *Journal of Education for Teaching*, 8, 2, 95–117.

Zeichner, K (1982) 'Reflective teaching and field-based experience in teacher education', *Interchange*, 12, 4, 1–22.

Chapter 2

The Developing Resource
Environment

Introduction

The concept of resources is defined in the Oxford English Dictionary as a 'means available to achieve an end'. In this chapter we will look at how a range of means can be classified as resources to help with your teaching and how you might research them. Existing and potential resources will be considered. We trust that you and your colleagues have a vested interest in researching the use of learning resources from a practical, pedagogical and philosophical perspective as part of your wider understanding of educational issues. The aim is to look at the different elements of the resource environment and to adopt a variety of approaches to the options on offer.

Background

The traditional resource environment in further and higher education has consisted of the library and textbooks. At one time, not too many years ago, the provision of an indicative or even a full bibliography of texts to consult in the library might have represented the only suggested resources. With the development of computer facilities, audio-visual and multimedia resources, the environment is much richer and more complex.

In this book, we suggest that learning resources are whatever can be defined as facilitating the learning process. Learning space, support staff and teaching staff all play an important role in the learning environment, as well as the physical learning materials. A listing of these would include the traditional print sources of books and journals, slides and photographs, audiotape, video, practical kits, remote databases and telecommunication systems including the Internet, e-mail, teleconferencing and satellite TV. Other resources include museums, art galleries, local industry, invited experts and people (for instance, as sources of oral history).

The resources environment has seen dramatic change over the last couple of decades and may change beyond recognition in the future. The Follett report (1993) offers three imaginary illustrations of some of the possibilities opened up by the technology of the 'virtual library'. In a virtual library, all information would be held electronically. Students could sit at one terminal and in theory have direct access to all the information they require which could be stored, accessed and transmitted electronically. Traditional publishing based on hard-copy books and journals is replaced by electronic publishing. The report suggests this would mean:

> the actual storage of knowledge – the articles, text, interactive experiences – had been passed back to its creators in the universities and elsewhere, to be retrieved, reformatted into the house style, and delivered to whoever ordered it. (Follett, 1993, p.69)

There are various educational technologies which might emulate some aspects of the teacher's role in student learning, but this enormous potential in the development of educational technology should be seen in the context of the aims and objectives of teachers and students. It should be appropriate to their needs; for instance, communication between students and teaching staff could be mediated by computer applications. Students could e-mail their essays and have them sent back with corrections in the electronic margins.

We subscribe to the ideal of the reflective practitioner when it comes to approaching teaching and learning objectives. Authors such as Ashcroft and Griffiths (1989) develop this further. In terms of learning resources it means being flexible in looking at the opportunities available, clear in the use of them and determined to think through the implications of their use. Heron (1981) has criticized academics who pride themselves on their ability critically to evaluate the assumptions on which a body of theory and practice is based, but who are uncritical and unthinking about educational processes.

Boyce (in Armsby *et al.*, 1987, p.547) recounts a stereotype of traditional further education teaching in the UK as:

> a lecturer, talk and chalk, teacher-centred, syllabus bound and exam orientated... benevolently despotic teacher control.... In trying to move away from the traditional teacher-dominated approach deep issues of educational philosophy as well as many practicalities are raised.

We intend to give an introduction to some important issues underlying research into learning resources in this chapter but we cannot cover all we would wish. In order to research into any aspect of teaching and learning in further and higher education you will need a fully informed awareness of current movements and debates. As a teacher, you have two main sources of information: the data acquired from the students you teach and published information. We suggest the first research task you undertake is to begin to investigate what has been done and is being done by others in your field and that you read a range of books and articles giving a general overview (the references in this book should help) and then narrow down to concentrate on those which are specifically relevant to your own particular situation.

As Anderson (1990) stated, successful research is based on all the knowledge, thinking and research that preceded it. We endorse his view that a review of the literature is an essential step in the process of undertaking a research study, especially as the number of studies and amount of knowledge in each field has escalated. Research reviews can be presented as research activities in their own right. As such they are also eminently publishable.

RESEARCH TASK. LITERATURE REVIEW

Define the search you are about to undertake in a sentence or short paragraph. It is much easier to search for information if you are clear and specific about your interest. One example might be, 'What has been written on course design relating to [your subject]?' Another, more specific might be 'Has anything been written on the use of CD-ROM in [your subject]?'

Identify sources for this information. Your librarian should be able to help you. Anderson (1990) provides several chapters on this in his book and Clarke (1993) and Tseng (1996) are useful in describing particular resources for education. Your own library catalogue is a good place to start. It would be useful also to search the catalogues of major national collections to find details of relevant books. There are indexes devoted to describing educational research and you will find others specific to your subject field. The key educational databases are:

● International ERIC (includes the British, Canadian and Australian Education Indexes and the British Education Theses Index).
● ERIC, an American database which is international in its coverage.

You could also try the:

● Social Sciences Citation Index. *Current Research* is available in three parts – Social Sciences, Humanities and Sciences – and describes projects in the UK.

- *Dissertation Abstracts* gives details of research around the world, particularly in the US.

Some reference sources helpful in providing reviews include:

- *Encyclopaedia of Educational Research*;
- *Handbook of Research on Teaching*;
- *Review of Educational Research*.

Once you have identified relevant documents you should read them and summarize the main points of interest. It is important to do this as you go along and to keep good records of what you have read. A file of index cards is one way to do this. Create an abstract of each document read and page references to particularly useful sections. Copy and file the most important documents to fit them into your chosen pattern.

You might find that drawing a 'rich picture' helps in this classification. A 'rich picture' is created by free association of ideas around a given topic represented in diagrammatic form. The categories shown in Figure 2.1 emerged from a rich picture of an overview of research into learning resources. You will probably find that many pieces of research overlap these areas, but they can be entered into your scheme more than once.

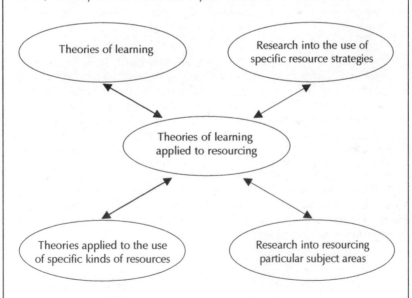

Figure 2.1 'Rich picture' diagram

Analyse the information you have gathered. Are you reading a review of research, an account of original research or official reports? Are the studies the result of analysis of systematically acquired data or the general experience of the authors? What research methodologies have been used? A wide range of approaches and presentation of research are valid but you need to understand the full context.

Write a review of information published on your chosen topic, tracing the development of any lines of research inquiry and evaluating any significance for your teaching practice. You may find it helpful to examine the influences of one researcher upon others, traceable through references and discussion in the texts. You might find that a researcher or a group of researchers emerges as so significant that your review could usefully concentrate on their work.

You might discover that others have already published a review very similar to what you propose. You may be able to build upon and develop their work.

Theories of Learning and Resources Provision

Before examining in detail specific resources and their research potential, the overall environment and its plethora of terminology needs some attention. When reviewing published material you may have noted values and assumptions about teaching and learning which are not critically evaluated.

Theories of learning can be broadly classified. In this chapter we discuss those that may be described as *behaviourist*, where the student is considered to be a passive recipient of teaching, or *cognitive*, where the student is considered to be an active participant in the learning process, which itself is characterized as the development and modification of cognitive structures. If you also introduce the ideas of the social context and motivation to the cognitive model, then we have a third classification often termed *socio-cultural theories*. Each of these groupings implies quite different aims and objectives for the learning process and would lead to different educational practice. A distinguishing element of the main schools of learning theory is the degree and type of control envisaged for the teacher. For a more detailed consideration of these theories see the discussion in Chapter 4.

Beard and Hartley (1984) have extracted 13 principles from the three psychological traditions which could be applied to the practice of teaching.

From *behaviourism* we have the principles of:

- activity – the learner is more effective when actively engaged;
- repetition – learning is improved through practice, particularly in multiple contexts;

- reinforcement – the reward of success improves learning and is the principal source of motivation.

From *cognitive theory* we have the principles of:

- learning with understanding – new knowledge should mesh with old;
- organization and structure – a logical structure of knowledge and sequencing of instruction improves learning;
- perceptual features – the form of presentation of information is important;
- cognitive feedback – learners should be given information on their progress;
- individual differences – intellectual ability and personality affects learning.

From *socio-cultural theory* we have the principles of:

- learning as a natural process – people have a natural curiosity;
- purposes and goals – defined goals increase motivation;
- social situation – group atmosphere affects learning;
- choice, relevance and responsibility – learning is improved when learners perceive relevance and are responsible for their own learning;
- anxiety and emotion – a threatening environment may inhibit learning, and learning will be more effective if it involves a student's emotions as well as intellect.

Applications of all these principles can be found in literature describing the development of curriculum planning in further and higher education. We are particularly interested in relating the use of resources to educational philosophy and we hope that at this point you are already beginning to see how you could investigate the application of theories such as these in your own situation.

RESEARCH TASK. INVESTIGATING THE PRINCIPLES OF LEARNING

This research task aims to enable you to identify ways in which these principles of learning might be observed in your course, particularly how they might affect the students' interaction with resources, and applied to improve the effectiveness of the course.

Take one of these principles; you might choose the principle of activity

– the learner is more effective when actively engaged. (For examples of active learning in practice see Race, 1992.)

You might like to use two groups – one a control group taught in your usual way, the other being provided in addition with self-assessment questions (SAQs).

Take an element of your course and one particular resource. In what ways are learners encouraged to become actively engaged? Can you identify problems associated with a lack of engagement?

Provide SAQs to accompany that resource to elicit a more active involvement with it.

Use your usual assessment techniques to measure any changes in students' understanding because of greater activity.

RESEARCH TASK. AN INVESTIGATION INTO THE EDUCATIONAL PHILOSOPHY OF AN INSTITUTION

Investigate the links between the explicit educational philosophy and the philosophy in practice within one or more institutions. We suggest that you might like to use two forms of data gathering for this investigation.

The first will be to list the formal expressions of educational philosophy gathered from such documents as institutional and departmental mission statements, course handbooks and prospectuses, course documentation and any material produced to inform academic staff, perhaps from staff development programmes. You should be able to produce a short report which summarizes the salient features of such documents.

The second is a survey of a sample of teaching staff designed to elicit their exposure to educational theory and their attitudes to such theories. You might like to use a series of one-to-one interviews in order to obtain detailed information. A number of ethical issues need to be carefully considered – particularly how you protect the privacy of individuals when they might be quite easily identified in a small setting. Anderson (1990) gives much useful guidance on conducting interviews and we suggest you adopt on this occasion the techniques known as an 'elite interview', which he describes. These are designed to: 'probe the views of a small number of elite individuals. An elite interview is one directed at a respondent who has particular experience or knowledge about the subject being discussed' (Anderson, 1990, p.223).

Interviewing requires much preparation and a certain amount of practice. You might like to find a partner to help you define the key issues for your particular situation. You need to work out a list of key questions but the advantage of an elite interview is that you can allow the conversation to develop as interesting lines of discussion emerge. A useful framework might be to list the principles of learning theory described by Beard and Hartley (1984), and to ask the interviewee to compare these first to their own philosophy and then to the institutional philosophy as they perceive it.

Write up the results of your interviews comparing and contrasting that information with formal institutional policy. Make a special note of the constraints on philosophy in practice, including resource issues.

Influences on the Resource Environment

In this section we consider three influences on the resource environment: developments in curriculum theory, changes in modes of course delivery, and advances in the range and sophistication of potential resources.

Armsby *et al.* (1987) provide a useful review of curriculum developments, relating them to resources provision, particularly in further education. It is interesting that they identify external factors such as funding constraints as equally important as educational philosophy. They note the following key trends:

- Pressure by funding bodies for increased efficiency leading to reduced class contact time.
- Moves towards student-centred learning requiring a more active student role in the acquisition of knowledge.
- Moves toward the lecturer becoming a facilitator of learning rather than just a deliverer of information.
- A wider range of teaching strategies being employed, such as project work and more integrated assignments.
- Study skills and core skills (numeracy, literacy, computer literacy and communication) as well as personal development to include self-reliance and critical awareness being required and enhanced by these learning styles.

They note that teaching methods in further education are moving towards a style that has until now been regarded by many as appropriate only to students in higher education, and suggest that students are being encouraged to become independent learners, finding out for themselves. They recommend that, in following such a model, the students should be equipped with the research and study skills which allow them to do this and with a range of resources to explore and learn from. They note that current teaching strategies encourage students to experiment with the information they find, reworking the information in various ways through discussion, presentations and project work in order that they can deeply understand concepts rather than repeating ideas parrot fashion.

Curriculum Design

Laurillard (1993) provides many practical suggestions for improving curriculum design and also researching the issues involved. The context is that of educational technology, but the approaches taken are more widely applicable (see Chapter 6 for further discussion of some of these ideas). The issues she raises to do with the design of learning materials are of relevance to our discussion here. She writes:

> The design of learning materials for any medium should always begin with the definition of objectives and analysis of student learning needs. Objectives will usually be given via some kind of curriculum design process that determines what students need to know or be able to do for a particular subject area. The objectives are defined in terms of the topic – the perceived priorities and values from the academic's point of view – without reference to the student, but rather thinking in terms of future learning needs, and the skills they wish to foster in their graduates. (Laurillard, 1993, pp.181–2)

The analysis of student learning needs involves discovering what position the student will be in at the beginning of the course in relation to these objectives, determining how to establish if they have reached the desired condition at the end and identifying where difficulties are likely to arise. In all these an awareness of the processes involved in student learning is required; these ideas are developed in Chapter 4. In the research task below we shall consider the first part of the design process: the definition of objectives.

RESEARCH TASK. DEFINING THE AIMS AND OBJECTIVES OF A COURSE

It is useful when planning a course to think in terms of *teaching aims*, which are a description of what you are trying to do, and *learning objectives*, which are specific targets, the achievement of which can be measured; for example:

Aim: to use the library effectively.
Objectives:
(a) students can locate a book on a particular subject in the catalogue
(b) students can find that book on the shelves.

The first stage is to determine the scope of your inquiry. You might like to take an overview of a range of courses or focus on a particular course, or even a single discrete assignment.

For each course or element, find out to what extent the objectives are defined in practice by external factors. Are the students working towards success in externally set examinations? If so, analyse how success would be measured by those examiners.

You might like to consider the following as elements of typical course objectives and compare them to the objectives of each course:

- The attainment of particular *subject-specific skills*. On some vocational courses these might take precedence over all other considerations. A hairdressing course, for example, will probably have as its main objective the attainment of specific skills relating to hair cutting, colouring and styling.
- The acquisition of *facts or information*. Courses will, to a greater or lesser extent, require students to memorize certain data. Car mechanics need to have a clear understanding of the workings of a vehicle, the processes of that system and how it might go wrong. They also need to be aware of legal constraints on their work, for example restrictions on emission levels.
- The acquisition of *academic knowledge*. This is probably the most complex area to investigate. Academic knowledge involves an understanding of abstract principles and concepts and an ability to reflect on this knowledge. There are three elements to this. The first is a growing awareness of key concepts; the second is a development of the student's skill in applying and transferring these concepts from one context to another; finally, the student will also be encouraged to question those concepts and develop critical independent judgement.
- The acquisition of *transferable skills*. These are information handling skills, study skills, analytic and presentational skills, etc which may be acquired through one particular course but are of benefit to the student in studying other courses or in a future career. (A major area of research is the question of whether more cognitive skills such as problem-solving are transferable from one domain to another. For an excellent review of research in this area, see Perkins and Salomon, 1989).

You might like to look, for comparison, at the discussion by Hake (1993) of the aims of initial teacher training.

Write up your research as a discursive paper on the constraints on particular types of course provision, and the extent to which these appear to be reflected in the elements included in course objectives.

Modes of Course Delivery

The language of student learning in relation to resources includes resource-based learning, distance learning, flexible learning, independent learning, student-centred and open learning, which all relate to modes of course delivery and all affect the resourcing strategy of a course. They are also characterized by a shift away from teacher-centred delivery, whether for reasons of economy or philosophical conviction.

We hope the following definitions will help but it is important to be aware that these terms are open to a variety of interpretations. As Savage (Armsby *et al.*, 1987, p.539) points out: 'Open learning is a term heard with increasing frequency in our institutions in recent years, yet there seem to be as many definitions of the term as people who use it'. The same is true of all the following terms which also seem to shade one into another and occasionally are used interchangeably. For a more detailed discussion of some of these terms, see Ashcroft and Foreman-Peck (1994).

Resource-based Learning (RBL)

RBL could be defined as a learning process in which the student uses a physical learning medium as the focus of the learning experience. In essence it involves an emphasis upon the tutor providing or directing students to resources they learn with, rather than the student receiving information directly from the teacher. Perhaps the most advanced realizations of this currently are computer programs which allow students to interact with them, asking questions, getting answers, with assessment built-in (see Chapter 4 for a discussion of the methods of evaluation of such resources). RBL has been seen as having the potential to replace teachers by the supposedly cheaper alternative of computer programs and workbooks. It may be more usefully described as a constructive re-evaluation of the processes of learning, allowing tutors to spend precious contact time effectively rather than delivering information through lectures which could be better conveyed through handouts and worksheets. This contrasts with the traditional higher education teaching methods of lectures, tutorials and essay writing supported by a library containing books and articles to which students are often directed by way of reading lists.

Each of the definitions given above may usefully form the subject of enquiry, particularly if you have already established that a commitment to RBL characterizes your institution.

RESEARCH TASK. INVESTIGATE HOW RBL COULD BE AN APPROPRIATE OPTION FOR ALTERING THE SHAPE OF YOUR COURSE

Choose an existing element of your course which you are delivering through lecture, seminar and essay-based work.

Analyse the structure of that element of your course in terms of:

- defined aims and objectives;
- identification of student learning needs;
- design of learning activities.

(See Laurillard, 1993, for an approach to such an analysis.)

Interactivity will exist between you and your students. Consider how this can be developed to promote interactivity between the students and the resources you use. You might consider:

- Ways of transferring information given verbally to printed hand-outs. Can you construct guides to learning based on your existing notes? How can you ensure these are read and understood?
- Ways of introducing interactivity to resources you are currently using. Could writing a set of student activities to accompany a particular resource improve their comprehension of the topic?
- Identifying which elements of the course are inappropriately delivered through RBL. Can selective use of RBL free your contact time for these activities? Can it give you time to spend with individual students who are experiencing difficulties?

Having identified potentially useful applications of RBL, experiment with their introduction:

- use a course evaluation questionnaire to establish students' reactions to these methods (see Ashcroft and Palacio, 1996, for methods of evaluation);
- evaluate through your usual methods of assessment the effectiveness of the technique in terms of student achievement of the goals of the course;
- assess the extent that it has benefited you, as the teacher. How much time was involved and was that an investment, because the resources could be reused? Did you feel that you were moving too far from the centre of the learning experience?

Write up this research task. It could be possible to do a compare and contrast exercise with a colleague to increase the validity of any findings.

You might like to read some of the series, 'Course design for resource based learning' (1994) produced by the Oxford Centre for Staff Development at Oxford Brookes University, UK, which relate to your subject area for comparison.

Distance Learning

Distance learning involves you in removing the constraints of time and place from a learning programme. It is usually characterized by the distance of the student from a physical campus. The Open University in the UK is a classic example. The Open University has in-house resources of very high quality which contain the bulk of the information needed by the students. They are designed to be interactive and often include books with questions at the end of each chapter, to encourage students to think about the material in a way which would normally be facilitated by tutorials or group discussion. Distance learning is 'open' in an administrative sense in that one set of constraints have been removed – the need to attend a course at specific times at a specific place. This enables students to study who would otherwise be restricted by the demands of full-time employment and/or family responsibilities.

Open Learning

Savage uses the Council for Educational Technology definition of open learning:

> courses flexibly designed to meet individual requirements. It is often applied to provision which tries to remove barriers that prevent attendance at more traditional courses, but also suggests a learner-centred philosophy…. In nearly every case specially prepared or adapted materials are necessary…. Students or clients are not asked to fit into provision already made in the college but in effect have a course constructed around and specifically for them. (Armsby *et al.*, 1987, p.539)

Students tend to learn through supported self-study. Open learning courses may be resourced through study packs which students work through on their own, or they may be supported by drop-in centres where students can work through resources they choose for themselves with assistance from subject specialists as required.

Open learning has also been defined by Boot and Hodgson (1987) as open in educational style. In adult and professional education particularly, open learning can mean that the student gains control over their own learning process, not only in terms of when and where they study, but in the extent to which the information they bring to a study group is valued in learning facilitated by the tutor rather than disseminated by him or her. For further discussion of the differing interpretations of open learning, see Bennett *et al.* (1996).

Flexible Learning

Flexible learning is similar to open learning in that the style of learning is designed to accommodate student preferences. Modular courses in which students can pick from a menu of options to design their own course are one manifestation of flexibility. Flexibility may also be seen, for example, in freedom of choice in topics or assignments, in the format for submitting work (presentations, group work, etc) and in methods of assessment (self- and peer assessment being options). Wright (1982) describes the Independent Studies degree at Lancaster University which gives students the opportunity to work out for themselves what subject areas and topics they wish to pursue and the ways and means by which they will pursue them. Boyce (in Armsby *et al.*, 1987, p.548) quotes Cornwall's suggestion that:

> there are six hierarchical stages towards student autonomy in which the learner successively determines:
>
> 1. The decision to enrol;
> 2. The pace of study;
> 3. The mode of study;
> 4. The study objectives;
> 5. The assessment methods;
> 6. The criteria for success.

The truly autonomous learner has total control over their learning. The best self-directed learning would satisfy these criteria but all courses might incorporate some degree of flexibility. Savage has pointed out that all open learning courses are student-centred, but other forms of curriculum delivery may be student-centred, encouraging student autonomy and self-direction. Associated is the idea of creating a lifelong interest in education by encouraging individual curiosity and a love of learning. Wright (1982) discusses this concept in some detail. One could also see a student-centred approach as being one that considered the experience of the course from the point of view of the student rather than the teacher.

Developments in Resources

The speed of change in new technology in recent years has widened significantly the resource options available to tutors, and the need to assess their effectiveness. What follows is a view of some of these possibilities and their resource potential.

The Internet

Highways for Learning (NCET, 1995) is very useful when considering the potential of the Internet. It contains a bibliography and list of contact addresses, provides an overview of how the Internet is currently being used and suggests potential developments. Although, as it says, 'The Internet itself, like paper or a CD-ROM, is a carrier of information and what it carries in 1995 does not yet provide resources tailored to the specific needs of UK teachers and learners' (p.11), the Internet has exciting potential and there are many research projects investigating ways in which it can be used constructively. For example, the Open Journals Framework Project in the UK has published on the Internet 'A survey of science, technology and medicine on-line journals 1990–95' which evaluates full-text, peer-reviewed journals.

One of the major problems with using the Internet is in locating useful information without spending hours following frustrating dead-ends. If your students' time is to be effectively employed on the Internet, you will find it useful to be able to direct them quickly to the resources you have identified as being relevant (see Chapter 4 for a discussion of different ways of providing guidance). You may also wish to protect them from offensive and pornographic material. You could consider setting up different levels of password controlled access.

We suggest the following research task based on setting up a 'home page', as one which will enable you to gain familiarity with use of the Internet; it will also be of practical use. A home page can serve two functions. It can provide a menu of the most useful sites on the Internet for your use and can also provide a site for any material you wish to make available to others, such as information about your courses and any research findings you wish to share with others. It can include an e-mail address so that you can work collaboratively with others and build connections.

You should ensure that your home page supports any house style of your institution and is approved by that institution. Your institution may also support you in the technical aspects of this endeavour. Tseng (1996) is one of many useful books now available to give you further information. You will need specific hardware and software and, especially initially, technical support.

RESEARCH TASK. CREATING A 'HOME PAGE' ON THE INTERNET

Familiarize yourself with the software necessary to access the Internet. 'Netscape' is one common and efficient software package available. The Internet can be searched either through 'search engines' which allow keyword searching, or through a browsing approach using the subject indices provided by various organizations. Internet software such as Netscape enables you to mark any useful sites with 'bookmarks'. The Internet is also particularly useful in connecting with organizations and people through on-line discussion and mailing lists.

Using HyperText Mark-Up Language (HTML) lets you provide direct links to useful resources as the student clicks on a highlighted word or phrase. Having identified a number of useful resources, you could develop a taxonomy of the resources, perhaps in the form of a subject tree. You might find it helpful to look at how other institutions have dealt with this. Resources can be divided by subject area or by kind. You might wish to provide direct links to specific useful resources and organizations, links to a range of search engines and a listing with addresses of relevant discussion groups. You might wish to provide links to guidance on the course objectives of using a particular resource or you might prefer to prepare a selection of these to distribute to students at the start of particular activities.

Once created, a home page needs attention if it is to remain useful as sites move and new resources come on-line. You need to build in systems for this updating. Perhaps students can be encouraged to inform you if they experience problems and you can set up a feedback e-mail channel for users of your home page. You might like to investigate ways in which you can be informed of useful new resources. Joining specific discussion groups can help in this. You might like to consider ways in which the results of individual exploration of the Internet in your institution can be pooled. Can you publicize your role in this?

Write up your experience of this as an article. You might like to adopt the 'story' technique, making it clear that the article reflects how you as an individual experienced the process. Keeping a detailed diary of developments can provide you with the data.

Multimedia

This term dates from the 1970s and originally meant the use of several media devices in a coordinated fashion. Now, with the advances in technology, it is more often used to describe multiple forms of information available from a single device. A single computer, perhaps using a CD-ROM, can provide access to text, graphics, sound, animation and video material at the same time.

An implementation of multimedia is that known as hypermedia. Hypertext was coined to mean non-linear arrangements of text, and essentially has come to mean sets of links from a computer screen to information in a database, thus allowing the interrelation of texts. Hypermedia is the extension of this idea to include multimedia resources. It covers computer-based material with links that allow the user non-sequential access to text, pictures, sound, etc. For example, a map may be displayed on the screen which has links to pictures and text about places on the map (for more information see Barker, 1993).

Hypermedia allows topics to be explored in multiple ways and the concepts involved to be used in different ways in different situations, thus contributing to flexible, integrated, inter-connected knowledge structures. This flexibility of representation of knowledge is felt to match the nature of realistic complex situations.

The original hypermedia systems allowed the student to search and browse established databases, structured by the authors by their use of links. Newer developments of this idea (see for example Scardamalia *et al.*, 1989) allow learners to add information and construct links themselves. This activity is similar to the process by which the learner normally constructs relationships in their own memory, and it is hoped that the explicit model of information representation created by the systems (perhaps enhanced symbolically with graphical node and link diagrams) may help the learner with their own mental models. For a good review of research into learning processes in the context of different media use see Kozma (1991).

The advantages of such systems for some learners may be disadvantages for others. The non-linear nature of hypermedia requires the student to decide for themselves what to look at and in what order. Newcomers to a domain or students with a particular style of learning may need some structure and guidance as to how to approach the information and knowledge being presented. We will discuss these ideas further in Chapter 4. The learner may become confused and get lost in the complexity of interconnections available in the learning environment and so some form of aid to navigation may be required. This is an idea we will develop in Chapter 6.

Conferencing

Conferencing or teleconferencing is a means of carrying out a discussion when the participants cannot meet face-to-face. We can draw a distinction between two types. On the one hand we have synchronous conferencing, where participants use the system at the same time, as with audio conferencing, using the telephone, or video conferencing. This is usually used to overcome logistical problems of distance between, say, the tutor and a dispersed group of students. On the other hand we have asynchronous conferencing, where participants use the system at different times. This is usually computer conferencing with facilities for organizing, storing and displaying messages sent by the members of the conference. This can be used to overcome the logistical problems of distance as well, but it also copes with the situation when the participants are not available at the same time.

Benefits claimed for computer conferencing, over and above that of liberating the participants from the constraints of time and place, are that it may encourage the less confident members to contribute and that, as there is time for reflection, the responses will be more considered and so the standard of debate will be higher. However, possible drawbacks to computer conferencing are that the subtlety of verbal communication is lost and that it can lack spontaneity. All these could be fruitful areas for research.

The technologies involved in conferencing can also be used for other forms of distance learning. Links to databases and video libraries facilitate on-line education and there is scope for the delivery of course material. An area of research here would be the experiences and attitudes of students undertaking this mode of course delivery. For further discussion of research into student needs, see Chapter 5.

Traditional Learning Resources

With so much change in the learning resource landscape and so many new features inhabiting it, there can be a tendency to forget, discard, or even ridicule older resources as outdated, outmoded, inefficient and not 'consumer friendly'. This would be unfair, unwise and wasteful of a wealth of valid resources. Just as cinema did not displace theatre, television did not displace radio, computers did not displace books, so it is with older forms of resource provision. You may need to see certain resources through new eyes and adopt different approaches. That can be an invigorating and fruitful exercise in its own right.

What follows is a consideration of traditional learning resources for your students, many of which we will return to in later chapters to look at how they can be researched from a specific teaching or student perspective.

Reading Lists

The reading list consists of a collection of books and articles selected by the tutor for dissemination to their students for use when studying (possibly including a set text). It may be used for background readings, preparing material for seminars and tutorials and for completing set assignments.

Courses of quality generally need a reading list of some sort to act as a starting-point for the uninitiated, a confidence-builder for the wary and a path to proceed down for the committed. At worst they can be an out-of-date list of dubious relevance drawn up some time ago, and perhaps added to, of titles with some vague relevance to the course, and from which students will discern what they can. At best they can be structured, relevant, up-to-date guides, with annotations to the titles in which their role and usefulness is made clear.

Consider the criteria you use when drawing up a list and how much discussion with students, if any, there is about it. The extent of its use, the effectiveness or otherwise of that use and the assessment of it, can all be areas for research.

Projects

A project is usually a particular task or assignment set for an individual or group to work on with a view to producing an end-product which relates, defines or clarifies a set of information on a particular topic in a formalized way, such as through a portfolio.

They can be clearly defined and articulated tasks with appropriate criteria and instructions, or they can be completely open-ended tasks set to encourage individual or group effort on a theme or issue being studied. The process of project work is research-based and the outcome can be a resource itself. The attitudes of various groups or types of student to different forms of project could make an interesting focus for enquiry.

If you set project work, consider how structured or open-ended it is and the extent of the advice you give. How far you expect other resources to be used is significant.

Laboratories

Originally a laboratory was a name given to a chemist's workroom where experimental work or research took place. It can still be that but it can also describe any place in which a series of activities are taking place in a controlled environment for the purpose of eliciting new information and findings on the subject matter in question, or confirming through a series of processes the accepted and acknowledged state of affairs. Laboratory work with students can be at the cutting edge of new knowledge or the reaffirmation of existing principles through experimentation and practice. The laboratory as a learning resource is worth researching.

Audio-visual Media

Audio-visual media involve the use of sound and/or vision as a means of presenting information. They are a widely used source for learning, particularly through the ubiquitous video-tape, audio-cassette and slide projection (see Ashcroft and Foreman-Peck, 1994, for more detail on types and uses of audio-visual aids). Video can be expensive to create and this can lead to an assumption of its worthiness; this may well be valid, but you might wish to research it more deeply.

Libraries and Other Contacts

There is a need to be able to access, interpret and evaluate a range of written and pictorial reference material. For instance, good libraries invest in a large selection of relevant journals to support learning in their institution. These can provide up-to-date information and analysis on a range of issues and are a potentially vital tool in supporting substantive and relevant work on the part of the student. Their cost is usually high, but necessary for academic respectability and intellectual integrity. They can be researched in terms of criteria for selection, analysis of the material within them and validity for a differentiated student intake.

There is a whole range of potential contacts that may become learning resources for students, such as museums, theatres and art companies, Industry Educational Units/Centres, local councils, government departments such as environmental and health, embassies, voluntary organizations, and outside speakers from many backgrounds.

Summary

In this chapter we discussed a flexible and wide-ranging series of approaches to explore the resource environment, looking at actual and potential opportunities. The next chapter will seek to place these in an institutional framework which looks at current and possible systems by which the changing environment can be best managed.

Annotated Reading List

Brewer, J G (1988) *Guidelines for Learning Resources in Colleges,* Ely: Peter Francis.
A useful guide to looking at learning resources which includes the results of a major UK survey.

Follett, B (Chairman) (1993) *Joint Funding Council's Libraries Review Group: Report,* Bristol: Higher Education Funding Council for England.
An extremely important milestone in the strategic planning of information provision for education in the UK, which potentially has wider international implications.

Oxford Centre for Staff Development (1994) *Course Design for Resource Based Learning Series,* Oxford: Oxford Brookes University.
Series produced by Gibbs *et al.* which looks at a range of case studies of RBL use in a number of disciplines.

References

Anderson, G (1990) *Fundamentals of Educational Research,* London: Falmer Press.

Armsby, A, Savage, P, Boyce, L, Leach, C, Evans, C, Davies, L and Chambers, F (1987) *Library and Learning Resources Management: Current Trends,* Bristol: Further Education Staff College.

Ashcroft, K and Foreman-Peck, L (1994) *Managing Teaching and Learning in Further and Higher Education,* London: Falmer Press.

Ashcroft, K and Griffiths, M (1989) 'Reflective teachers and reflective tutors: school experience in an initial teacher education course', *Journal of Education for Teaching,* 15, 1, 35–52.

Ashcroft, K and Palacio, D (1996) *Researching into Evaluation and Assessment in Colleges and Universities,* London: Kogan Page.

Beard, R M and Hartley, J (1984) *Teaching and Learning in Higher Education,* New York: Harper and Row.

Barker, P (1993) *Exploring Hypermedia,* London: Kogan Page.

Bennett, C, Foreman-Peck, L and Higgins, C (1996) *Researching into Teaching Methods in Colleges and Universities,* London: Kogan Page.

Boot, R and Hodgson, V (1987) 'Open Learning: Meaning and Experience', in Hodgson, V, Mann, S and Snell, R (eds) *Beyond Distance Teaching: Towards Open Learning,* Milton Keynes: Open University Press.

Clarke, P (1993) *Finding Out in Education: A guide to sources of information,* Harlow: Longman.

Follett, B (Chairman) (1993) *Joint Funding Council's Libraries Review Group: Report,* Bristol: Higher Education Funding Council for England.

Hake, C (1993) *Partnership in Initial Teacher Training: Talk and chalk,* London: Institute of Education.

Heron, J (1981) 'Assessment revisited', in Boud, D (ed.) *Developing Student Autonomy in Learning,* London: Kogan Page.

Kozma, R (1991) 'Learning with media', *Review of Educational Research*, 61, 2, 179–211.

Laurillard, D (1993) *Rethinking University Teaching: A framework for the effective use of educational technology*, London: Routledge.

National Council for Educational Technology (NCET) (1995) *Highways for Learning*, Coventry: NCET.

Oxford Centre for Staff Development (1994) *Course Design for Resource Based Learning Series*, Oxford: Oxford Brookes University.

Perkins, D and Salomon, G (1989) 'Are cognitive skills context bound?', *Educational Researcher*, 18, 16–25.

Race, P (1992) *53 Interesting Ways to Write Open Learning Materials*, Bristol: Technical and Educational Services.

Scardamalia, M, Bereiter, C, McLean, R, Swallow, J and Woodruff, E (1989) 'Computer-supported intentional learning environments', *Journal of Educational Computing Research*, 5, 51–68.

Tseng, G (1996) *The Library and Information Professional's Guide to the Internet*, London: Library Association.

Wright, J (1982) *Learning to Learn in Higher Education*, Beckenham: Croom Helm.

Chapter 3

Setting the Institutional Framework for Research and Learning

Introduction

In this chapter we relate the issues raised in the last chapter on learning resources and curriculum planning and policy to the institutional framework. We will outline some possible investigations into the organization of learning resources provision in colleges and universities, including into management strategies which may facilitate development in this field. We look at the various learning resources departments within an institution and the ways in which staff – academic, support and para-academic – may be involved in resource provision. We will draw on theories of management to suggest models for constructive research into the resource environment.

Structure and Culture: A Context of Change

The institutional context in which you are researching the development of learning resources is almost invariably going to be one of great change. In the previous chapter we began to discuss how teaching and learning in post-16 education is changing. In discussing the changes in the resources environment we identified three significant influences: developments in curriculum theory, advances in the range and sophistication of potential resources, and funding constraints causing greater student-to-staff ratios. Other factors which can be identified include a changing student profile with an increase in mature students, increased expectations from students as they become more self-financing, and more explicit demands from funding bodies that institutions address priorities set by government policy.

Phillips (in Slowey, 1995, Appendix) provides a clear summary of UK government policy as it has affected further and higher education. The key points are:

- In the UK, policy has been to expand dramatically post-16 education since 1987, without significantly increasing the proportion of the national budget to fund it. Institutions have seen increases in student numbers but a fall in funding per student. Phillips notes that the biggest growth is recorded in colleges and the former polytechnics, which welcomed increased numbers because they supported a policy of widening educational opportunity and also sought to increase their funding, heavily reliant at that time on income from teaching. The universities were more cautious in bidding for extra numbers 'concerned at the effect of declining funding per student on the quality of teaching and at the effect of increased student numbers on research quality' (Slowey, 1995, p.164). Colleges, former polytechnics and universities have all seen a reduction in per capita funding but the pressure of increased numbers is generally felt most keenly in colleges and the former polytechnics.
- This period has also seen government policy encourage wider access for non-traditional students, mature students and part-time higher education for those in employment. The increase in student numbers was achieved by greater numbers across all age groups, but particularly mature students.
- The government has introduced various measures to monitor quality of teaching and research since the 1987 White Paper, 'Higher education: meeting the challenge' which set out the government's agenda to see 'improvements in the design and content of courses and in quality of teaching'. Universities had been largely self-regulating while standards at polytechnics and colleges were monitored by various validating bodies. Quality assessment was formalized across the sectors in the 1992 Further and Higher Education Act which requires the Higher Education Funding Councils to 'secure that provision is made for assessing the quality of education in those institutions for whose activities they provide, or are considering providing, financial support'. Assessments have involved a mixture of self-assessment and sometimes an institutional visit by a team of assessors. Another initiative has been the Higher Education Charter (DfE, 1992) which sought to establish minimum standards that students could expect.

Institutional Responses to these Pressures

Weil (1994) and Slowey (1995) both present a collection of 'stories' or personal accounts of the experiences of senior and middle managers in universities and colleges in the UK. The accounts reveal the diversity of the changes being experienced at the institutional level, the role ambiguity and conflicts of the academic as a manager and reflections on strategies adopted to implement change. We have picked out some of the interesting themes emerging from these stories. You may wish to consider which of these themes you can relate to what you have found in your own institution. You might like to consider whether a personal account of your experience, in the form of a story, would be an appropriate vehicle for disseminating it.

One of the most interesting issues which emerges from the case studies is the varying institutional support for the reflective practitioner. Laurillard has argued the importance of an institutional framework which fosters a reflective approach to teaching:

> Teachers need to know more than their subject. They need to know the ways it can come to be understood, the ways it can be misunderstood, what counts as understanding: they need to know how individuals experience the subject. But they are neither required nor enabled to know these things... education... is being forced to change... the pressure is for financial input to go down, and some measurable output to go up.... We need to rebuild the infrastructure that will find the fit between the academic values we wish to preserve and the new conditions of educating larger numbers.(Laurillard, 1993, p. 3–4)

Gibbs *et al.* echo these concerns. They write:

> Many of the case studies were presented at these conferences by isolated individuals fighting a hostile and obstructive system.... Frameworks have been evolved (rather than having been designed) over many years in universities and colleges which support conventional course delivery and delivery based on classroom teaching and library use. RBL uses teachers, accommodation and learning resources in new ways, and many features of institutional infrastructures block developments in RBL. (Gibbs *et al.*, 1994, p.5)

On the other hand, many of the personal accounts given by senior managers in Weil (1994) and by middle managers in Slowey (1995) in their analysis of managing innovation and change highlight problems in persuading academic staff of the need to change and cooperate. Thorley (in Slowey, 1995, p.58) felt that 'managing academics is akin to herding cats'. Todd describes the strategic issues facing institutions and curriculum managers very clearly:

Only the management staff of colleges can assemble the financial base and the strategy required to provide the learning environment appropriate to curriculum delivery involving less class contact and larger classes than have been traditionally represented in the further education delivery model. Only lecturers can devise and implement coherent curriculum models which integrate all forms of student learning. (Todd, in Slowey, 1995, p. 125)

One could add that it would also be appropriate wherever possible to involve resource managers, including the resource centre and computer centre staff, in supporting a learning environment. Todd presents a classic story of curriculum management in response to the pressures of an expansion in further education. The expansion involves a declining unit of resource and therefore increases in class size and reduction in teacher contact time with their class. The response by Newcastle College was to modify curriculum delivery models to ensure that structured learning opportunities were provided outside class contact time through library-based study, small group activity and other forms of learning.

It seems that representatives from the academic side and from those responsible for managing the institution recognize the necessity of responding to change productively. Even specific developments necessary to implement curriculum changes which will permit expansion of numbers without compromising quality are seen to be generally accepted. In these circumstances you may wonder why it is felt that universities and colleges are not able to adapt to change smoothly.

Universities and colleges are not only facing imperatives to change but must find ways of doing this so that quality is preserved or even enhanced. Fundamental assumptions about educational management are being challenged. Several people have noted that traditional collegiate structures of management are coming under threat. Price notes that universities have traditionally been resistant to industrial management models (in Weil, 1994). The whole concept of a chief executive is viewed with suspicion. In many universities the role scarcely yet exists.

He describes a traditional structure in which an academic senate democratically decides what changes should be made and sets institutional policy. An administrator is in place to enact the decisions of the senate. He goes on to compare traditional university management with that prevailing in the former polytechnics of the UK which in effect had always had de facto chief executives who were not used to the possible obstructions within university collegiality. He also points out that further education institutions were once under more control from local political authorities who could act as an external adjudicator on controversial management decisions. Once polytechnics were removed from local authority control the directors were obliged to consider how to maintain the consent of staff alongside the management of change.

Webb describes the problems he faced as a manager of an academic department: on the one hand he was expected by the 'corporate centre of the university... to sign up to change and opportunities at very short notice' while 'back in the department... he was expected to conform to his colleagues' expectations of respect for their perceived position as self-directed professionals' (in Weil, 1994, p.42).

A recurrent theme is the conflict between the influence on the institution from external funding agencies which is felt most keenly by senior management, and the priorities of individual academics. Bull suggests that chroniclers would note the following in the late twentieth century history of higher education:

> A dominant theme might be the rise of educational consumerism, an
> analysis of the extent to which the previously grateful and largely
> passive, direct and indirect recipients of higher education – the
> student, the employer, industry, society – had shaped, influenced or
> even dictated the purposes of the once autonomous universities. A
> second might be the substitution by Government of explicit regulation
> by a doctrine of accountability – for funds, for quality, for consumer
> satisfaction – and the influence this too exerted upon institutional
> strategies and purposes. (Bull, in Weil, 1994, p.82)

Effective management – of an institution or of a specific project within that institution – relies on a clear and generally accepted set of goals and priorities as well as specific strategies for reaching them. Those goals must somehow effect a marriage between the priorities set by external funding agencies and those of the people working within that institution. Many people have pointed out how difficult it is to translate this into practice. Tann reported that heads perceive departmental colleagues to be overwhelmed with things to do and so unable to stand back from the day-to-day operational issues to contribute to planning for the future.

A crucial issue identified here is time. Tann notes that strategic management requires a balance between rapid responses and maximum staff involvement in the process. In the past committee structures could facilitate this, but many managers have pointed out that such procedures are simply too slow. Price (in Weil, 1994) suggests committees are a recipe for cultural arthritis and recommends the creation of dynamic teams. Bull (in Weil, 1994) describes universities as having two cultures which invite tensions. One is a bureaucracy, driven functionally by rules, procedures and structures most commonly found among administrative staff who have to implement systems which respond to the pressures for public accountability. The other is an organic or task culture which he associates with academics. He notes that this culture is essential if scholarship is to flourish but that it can degenerate into anarchy. Effective management must find some way of combining the two cultures into one organizational framework in which all staff share values which inform strategic and policy decisions and day-to-day operations. In this model rules constrain but are not the driving force.

Structure and Culture: Response to Change

The issue of change within an academic organization is an interesting one. Questions include: How does your organization respond to change? Is it seen as a threat or an opportunity? Are staff supported through change with retraining? Is change imposed top-down or by involving as many staff as possible? Is change always appropriate and justified or can it be due to the enthusiasm of a minority pulling the rest along? Change is inevitable but is it accommodated effectively?

In the rest of this chapter we will be looking at how you could investigate the structure and the culture of an institution and how it responds to change and, more particularly, how this affects the provision and development of learning resources. Structure is usually far easier to identify than culture. Structure is the formal pattern of an institution. Price (in Weil, 1994, p.37) describes it as a 'wiring diagram in the world of who reports to whom'. It could be a formal arrangement of departments and faculties, a hierarchy of committees or authorized individuals, or a loose confederation of planning teams. The culture of an institution is the attitudes of the people working within it and the atmosphere. Structure is usually a formal arrangement; culture might be seen in the informal relationships and individual responses within that structure.

Systems Analysis

In investigating culture and structure, a systems approach is one possible model to adopt. Underwood gives a very clear and readable introduction:

> The systems approach to management provides a framework and body
> of techniques for accomplishing change.... Change can offer

opportunities [as well as difficulties] and the systems approach
provides a means of encouraging managers to identify, investigate,
evaluate and promote such opportunities. (Underwood, 1990, p.4)

The key concept is that a systems approach recognizes the complexity
of an institution and seeks to identify the 'subtle balance of objectives,
tasks, personalities and events'. Components within that system can be
analysed, described and costed, their function can be defined and
understood, their performance can be evaluated. The manager can
experiment with new working methods or other changes, and monitor
effects. It is possible to schematize the workings of an institution through
the creation of system models. Systems analysis is a method of identifying
the components of any system and the dynamic interactions between
them. The workings of the system can be laid out in a diagrammatic
form, any part of which can become the focus of attention and ex-
panded. For example, an organization chart delineates the formal
structure of an institution's system. The system components will be the
individuals and groups of individuals which make up the institution,
influence each other and are in various ways also influenced by the world
outside. In investigating that system, a manager can take any part of it,
focusing attention on the effects of change on that sub-system, while
having the overall system to provide a full context. You might like to take
the structures supporting the provision and development of learning
resources in your organization and lay out the relationships in the form
of a model.

Resource provision frameworks may be based on top-down management or consensus. They may be essentially conservative or experimental. They might have a vision involving explicit policy targets, or not. The
purpose of the research task below is to gain some systematic understanding of the structure and culture of your institution. It would be
particularly useful if you could find a colleague who would be willing
to undertake a parallel study for comparison, ideally in a different
institution.

RESEARCH TASK. SYSTEMS ANALYSIS

Start by outlining in broad terms the components of the resourcing system
in your institution and linkages between them. Define the broad role each
component plays within the system. It might look something like Figure
3.1:

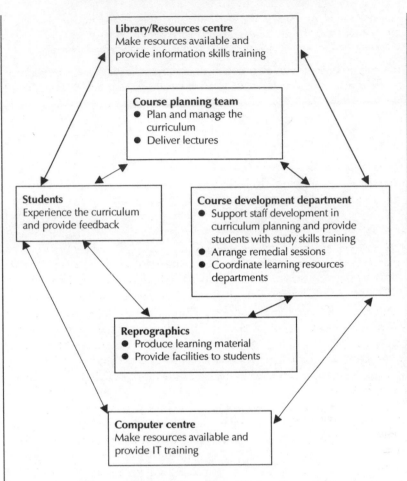

Figure 3.1 *Example outline of resourcing system*

Describe the channels of communication between students, resource-providers and course managers. You might come up with a variety of models for their relations and communications with each of the other components. It will probably be most illuminating to look in detail at the relationships formed by a department other than your own.

- Describe how the library or resource centre fits into the institution's structure.
- Analyse relationships between the library or resource centre and course-managers. Is the attendance of relevant staff at committee meetings significant?

- Look at the extent to which librarians and others responsible for managing learning resources are involved in decision-making and informed about developments within the academic environment.

Investigate the committee or deliberative structure; it may look like Figure 3.2. Each arrow represents a two-way process of information transferral. Discussion takes place and decisions are made in each box or passed to a superior body for approval. The decisions made are then passed down the chain of command and implemented at various levels. The flow of information can be impeded at any point.

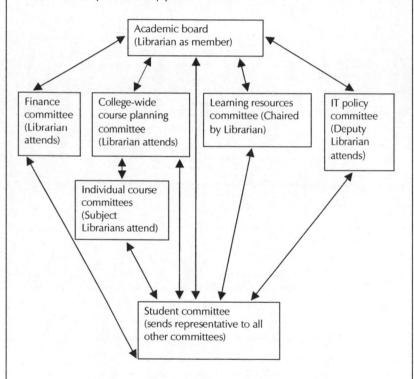

Figure 3.2 *Example of committee structure*

The committee structure is a common one in academic organizations but is not the only pattern of management that you might find. Sometimes decision-making is vested in individuals rather than committees and the patterns that emerge from your study will reflect this.

Look at formal documents produced by the institution. Many institutions have organizational charts you can refer to which will lay out the structures. Job descriptions, if they are available to you, will provide more detailed information about responsibilities and reporting structures. If you find that the institution does function through a committee structure, those meetings will usually be listed in some form of institutional diary, if only for room bookings. You might already be a member of various committees, or may ask for the minutes of the meetings to be circulated to you. You will probably need to interview key figures in the institution.

Having delineated your structure, track a specific issue as it is discussed by and affects the institution. You should choose a clearly defined and specific issue – one which has implications across the institution. Perhaps your institution is considering establishing an initiative to improve learning support for distance learners or students with dyslexia. If so, you might investigate the following:

- Where has the suggestion come from?
- Who acts upon it?
- How are decisions reached?
- Where does the money come from to do it?
- What are the blocks upon the project?

Write up the results of your investigation and accompanying schema with an emphasis on the uses of systems analysis. You might like to involve other staff in a discussion of the research results. Be very careful about the ethical dimension of this research. You are looking at the workings of an organization, but that organization is composed of people and the complex relationships between them, and it is very easy to upset people. Be very sure to test the waters with a tactful colleague before broadcasting your findings.

The institutional framework is often mentioned when new curriculum initiatives or resourcing strategies are described in the literature. The case study approach is a popular way of presenting specific situations or developments in educational institutions. You might like to present your findings in this form. Case studies can integrate and present data gathered through various methodologies. Anderson suggests that the case study:

> is a teaching document generally incorporating a chain-of-evidence borrowing from the techniques used in criminological investigation....
> Thus the case-study report... takes the reader along a similar path to the one the researcher has followed in coming to his or her conclusions.
> (Anderson, 1990, p.163)

He writes that case studies are often appropriate as a research method which is 'process-orientated, flexible and adaptable to changes in circumstances and an evolving context' such as that of 'a particular decision and how it was implemented...[or] the deliberations of a committee or other group of people' (see Anderson, 1990, and Yin, 1981, for more detail).

Although individual case studies do not permit much generalization, it is possible to analyse a collection of case studies for patterns and lessons learnt. You might find it helpful to read and analyse a range of case studies from other institutions before you embark on a case study in your own. The bibliography at the end of this chapter will give you a range of case studies to examine. You might also like to look at Brewer (1988) who includes the results of a survey of the organization of learning resources provision in the UK and a number of detailed case studies.

He found that the library is usually only one of several academic support departments within any institution providing learning resources. Library provision and computer centres are both well established in colleges and universities. Staff within media services and reprographics are developing a new role in many colleges, working with academic staff in the development of in-house production of resources both in print and in other media such as computer programs and video. Some departments have evolved to the status of publishing houses, making in-house productions commercially available. Related to these services, some institutions have curriculum development units which work with academic staff in curriculum design, staff development and perhaps resources production. They may focus staff development activity through conferences and workshops and may facilitate the development of new approaches to teaching. Another phenomenon has been the growth of dedicated learning support units which provide remedial assistance in, for example, study skills, mathematics, language skills, and IT skills or course-specific assistance to students. These may be set up with more or less input from academic staff. Some have set up dedicated learning centres attached to particular courses which provide key resources and equipment where the course is delivered.

The Institution as an 'Open System'

The body of systems theory also includes a variety of models which could, if found constructive, be adopted and applied to assist in strategic planning. Underwood (1990) describes a simple systems model for the institution as an open system relating to its environment; this is shown in Figure 3.3.

This model, when applied in formal institutional planning, is designed to ensure that the organisation is stimulated to respond to changes and develop constructively. Efficiency (economical use of resources) and effectiveness (meeting the goals of the organization) are regularly

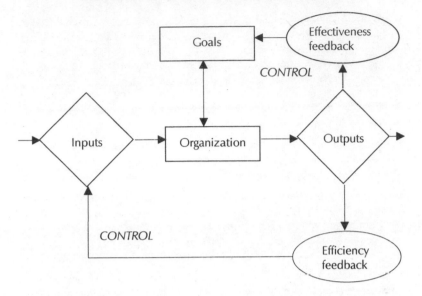

Figure 3.3 *Open system model (from Underwood, 1990, p.21)*

assessed through the establishment of feedback mechanisms. This model could also be useful when planning the implementation of a particular project. This might all sound very mechanistic and inhuman but it may be an aid to developing a 'reflective' or thinking and learning organization. Laurillard (1993) suggests that the academic system needs to find methods of learning and adapting to changes constructively through mechanisms which allow the monitoring of effectiveness. Shackleton (in Weil, 1994, p.109) describes developing strategic management as the 'need to stimulate and develop the college's capacity to think'.

RESEARCH TASK. INVESTIGATING THE ORGANIZATION AS AN OPEN SYSTEM

Take the open system model described in Figure 3.3 and apply it to the model of the learning resources organization you have delineated in the previous research task.

Consider the following points:

- What are the goals of the institution?
- Are they expressed in a mission statement?
- Is that mission statement supported by detail in explicit policy?

- Are the mission statement or goals widely understood and mirrored in statements for particular sub-systems such as learning resources departments?
- How far is the mission statement related to demands from the external environment such as funding agencies?
- How far is it related to the demands/needs of the students?
- How far does it reflect the educational philosophy of the academic staff?

Relate the concepts of feedback mechanisms for effectiveness and efficiency to the workings of the system. For example you might find that there are specific blocks in the transmission of vital management information.

- Are there procedures for student feedback at all relevant places in the system?
- Identify procedures for disseminating information about the external demands on the system (for example funding directives).
- Establish the extent to which effort in collecting information at one place is duplicated at another.

Find out whereabouts in the system specific decisions are made in response to feedback and how those decisions are implemented throughout. Ask whether the results of those decisions are monitored for effectiveness. The two processes of decision-making and information circulation are crucial to the success of any organization. You are likely to discover aspects of the system that are effective and others which are not.

Having made your own investigation you might like to adopt the approach of a focus group to develop your ideas. Anderson (1990) provides a very useful chapter on the use of focus groups to gather information, and Ashcroft et al. (1996) take you step by step through the process of using focus groups in educational research. Make sure you include in your focus groups people from various parts of the organization. Choose several academic staff, several senior managers if you can, some students, and people to represent learning resources departments and administration. You will need to prepare the questions carefully and may wish to ask another colleague to help you record what happens. It is difficult to direct discussions and take notes at the same time.

Ask the group to consider the points and questions shown above.

Write up the results of your investigation relating your findings back to the open systems model.

- What have you learnt?
- Can you offer practical suggestions to other curriculum managers who may wish to develop the reflective management of their institution?
- What needs to be done to enhance links within the institution for the benefit of students?
- Has the project itself improved communication?

Interpersonal relationships can influence decision-making much more than formal reporting structures. Perhaps the institutional manager has little faith in the librarian and is not willing to invest in library services because he or she does not trust that the investment would be wisely managed. On the other hand, a librarian who is perceived as a good manager may find their role developing into a much broader cross-college management role. The effectiveness of communication between academic subject teams and their colleagues in the learning resources department can depend very much on compatibility of temperament and perceived shared values. An academic environment is a complex one – and very fluid as staff come and go. Pockets of activity may centre around energetic staff. Staff may identify with their department rather than the institution, or with students, and this may affect the way they view change.

RESEARCH TASK. SWOT ANALYSIS OF THE RELATIONSHIPS BETWEEN ACADEMIC STAFF AND RESOURCE STAFF AT YOUR INSTITUTION

A SWOT analysis is an investigation of the strengths, weaknesses, opportunities and threats of a given situation. You might use this model in a group brainstorm including academic and resourcing staff. The goal is to improve communication between departments and to discover more effective ways of utilizing the particular strengths of staff involved. According to Underwood (1990), strengths and weaknesses refer to factors which can be controlled or influenced by the organization or particular department, opportunities and threats refer to factors over which the organization may not have any direct control or influence. You could focus on an issue and analyse the relationships revealed by the discussion, but it would be more ethical and perhaps more constructive to use the issue itself as a discussion point. You might come up with several models outlining the situation as perceived by each department and an overview of the integrated SWOT analysis.

A very simple example, focusing on IT staff, might look like Figure 3.4.

- How can you make use of this research project in practical ways? Could staff development activities be used to raise awareness of techniques to improve communication and team working?
- What practical knowledge do staff have to help them understand and use group dynamics?
- What factors can be used to highlight effectiveness in organizational relationships? Can efficiency in resource provision be related to communication between academic and support staff?

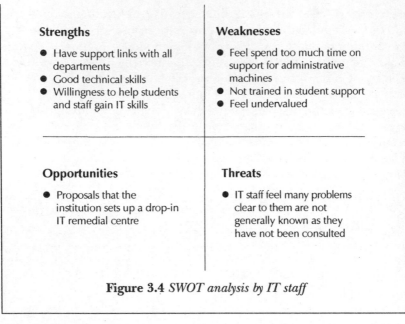

Figure 3.4 *SWOT analysis by IT staff*

Integration of Services

A feature of developments in learning resources provision in recent decades has been the move in many institutions to integrate various resource departments. Brewer (1988) found great variety in the arrangements of learning resources and in which department was amalgamated with which. A special issue of *Relay: The Journal of the University College and Research Group*, (no.42, 1995) was devoted to an analysis of this phenomenon. You could investigate the extent to which learning resources are integrated in your institution and what effect there has been or could be on the quality of service provided. Specific issues which could be addressed include the efficiency of communication within a unified body, as opposed to the development of systems of better communication between departments. You could explore whether concentration upon specialism is more useful than a sharing of responsibilities: for example, the responsibility for the exploitation of networked information sources, such as CD-ROMS and the Internet, could be shared between the library and computer centre.

The Changing Role of Support Staff

The distinction between academic staff and support staff is becoming blurred. This can be seen, for example, in the case of librarians. It has been stated that,

> ...we need, above all, liberally educated librarians. Professionals who understand and are interested in undergraduate education, who are involved in educational matters and who can open the stocks to students, create browsing rooms, reference the reserve book system, help distribute books throughout the campus and expand holdings in ways that enrich the undergraduate experience. (Boyer, 1987, p.160)

It would be useful to analyse exactly how these roles are developing in order to investigate this phenomenon. The tutor or academic is usually responsible for the construction and delivery of a course. Individually, or more usually as a team, courses will be written, including assessment activities, lectures, tutorials, seminars and practical activities. The tutor will often prepare a more-or-less detailed list of resources to direct students to the required and suggested reading to back up the course. The librarian's role has been to acquire, organize and care for those learning materials and to ensure that tutors and students alike are able to find the materials they require. A significant development in most institutions has been the growth of 'user education' programmes delivered by library staff with greater or lesser coordination with academic staff. These grew out of the traditional library tour and often became detailed courses integrated into the main course structure. They are usually designed to equip the student with transferable information skills as well as provide specific orientation for the local collections. As electronic sources of information increase, such training has gained a much higher profile.

In this context the librarian's role has become to some extent a teaching one. If courses encourage students to find out for themselves from the widest range of resources available within the institution and outside, they will need enhanced information skills in order to locate material. They will also need to be able to evaluate that material for its appropriateness for their needs and to manipulate the information found. In some institutions, study skills training has been taken up by library staff as part of the courses they provide. Such skills include note-taking, revision, time management, essay planning,etc. Some institutions have established learning workshops – especially in further education – to help students with literacy, numeracy or study skills. These may be set up centrally, perhaps within a learning centre which also includes the library and computer centre and may be staffed by non-academic staff.

In looking at these developments, you might be faced with a number of potentially researchable questions: What is the teaching role of the librarian and other support staff? How far should support staff take advantage of potential learning situations for students? Should computer technicians teach students how to perform a particular task or restrict themselves to maintenance of the software available to the students? Which should take higher priority: maintenance of the institution's computer systems or assisting students with technical problems in word-processing? Should library assistants simply find books for students or should they teach students how to search the catalogue more effectively or suggest alternative sources of information?

Brewer (1988) found that resources support staff felt they had a lot to offer academic staff but were under-utilized. On the other hand, support staff, including librarians, may feel that they are being expected to adapt to new roles without adequate training or support. In some institutions, developments in resource-based learning might be perceived as a shifting of control from academic staff to resourcing staff, with understandable resentment. You might find it interesting to explore ways of maximizing existing staff strengths through cooperation, and in particular the specific skills pertinent to teaching staff and the various support staff, or how staff are experiencing change in their roles in your institution.

RESEARCH TASK. EXPLORING DIFFERENTIATED ROLES THROUGH SHADOWING

The purpose of this activity is to gain an understanding of the specific skills, interactions with students and contributions to the learning environment made by staff with different roles, with a view to discovering whether this growth in understanding can improve effectiveness in student support.

Arrange with a colleague for the opportunity for both to shadow the other in turns at pre-arranged times. Allow time to experience as full a variety of situations as possible. If this is not possible, then sharing of detailed diaries might offer a similar though limited experience.

For example, teaching staff might offer support staff the opportunity to observe lectures, seminars, fieldwork, tutorials, laboratory work, course planning and other meetings, marking and other assessment activities. Librarians might offer teaching staff the opportunity to observe formal information skills seminars; informal interaction with students at an enquiry desk; activity related to the management of resources, such as the ways

---

decisions are made in relation to the classification, description and location of resources and the development of databases including the local catalogue; library management and other meetings.

Write up an account of this experience. What have you learnt about specific skills employed? Has a greater understanding resulted in any specific benefits? Consider to what extent, if any, cross-training is beneficial. If the results are positive, use this experience as a pilot for a larger work-shadowing project, with the data collected in the form of reflective diaries that may be analysed using emergent categories (see Bennett et al., 1996, for more detail on how to go about this).

Another useful area to explore in a research task is the teaching of information and other study skills. Library staff are probably already delivering some kind of library skills course at your institution and you might like to explore the ways you can work together, using your differentiated skills, to make those courses appropriate to your students. You might like to explore the treatment by Reekie (1990) of a similar investigation. Anderson (1990) provides useful guidance in the context of programme evaluation.

RESEARCH TASK. EVALUATION OF THE EFFECTIVENESS OF INFORMATION SKILLS TRAINING

Conduct a telephone interview with library staff and tutors in a variety of institutions. Ask questions that cover the following general points:

- How far are formal training sessions tailored to the needs of students on particular programmes? Are they delivered in subject groups by a library subject specialist?
- To what extent does training focus on the facilities available locally and how far are transferable skills addressed? How far are those skills relevant to the aims and objectives of particular courses?
- Are the students given study skills training within the course or are these left to another agency?
- To what extent are tutors and librarians involved with the development and delivery of the course?
- Is there a particular vocabulary or taxonomy of ideas which students studying particular subjects will need to acquire?
- Is assistance with this provided within information skills sessions run by tutors or librarians, and if so what form does such assistance take?
- Are there subject-specific resources – a set of journal titles, archival materials, reference books, CD-ROM titles – that tutors or library staff emphasize to the students?

- Do course tutors expect students to research widely for themselves or are they directing their attention to specific resources? Does this change through the course as more independence is required?
- How far are students motivated to attend courses in information skills? Do tutors or library staff encourage students to attend? Do tutors accompany them? How is it timetabled – as a voluntary activity or part of their time allocated to formal instruction?
- How far is it integrated with course delivery? Is there any formal assessment of student understanding?
- Does the course emphasize hands-on practice? What kind of materials accompany the course? Is student feedback encouraged and how does that information affect the way the course develops? Does it meet the quality criteria established for other courses in your institution?

Write up your findings. Identify trends in information skills support or ways in which the information skills training could be improved.

Institutional Framework and Resourcing Strategies

There are funding constraints on the provision of resources within an institution, whether those resources are defined in terms of available cash, space, staff hours or library and other resources. The institution must compete with others for limited resources from funding agencies and in the attraction of students. Individual departments, including learning resources, must compete for funds within the institution. You might like to explore the criteria used by managers in resource allocation within your institution. How far are they influenced by explicit criteria expressed by funding agencies (including commercial sponsors), awareness of students' expressed or potential needs, or awareness of the perspectives of academic staff? You could explore also the extent to which senior managers' perceptions of individuals influence funding and the nature of the discussions relating to funding. You could look at which of the interested parties are allowed to express their opinions and the extent to which resource allocation is determined by the relative profitability of courses.

The Follett report (1993) called for resource allocation methods for libraries which were both transparent and able to foster clear accountability. It suggests that library objectives should be clearly related to the allocation of resources to meet them. Gibbs *et al.* (1994) call for more efficient course costing, and claim that many factors, such as library and laboratory costs and student drop-out and failure, are ignored because they are deemed to be impossible to calculate or irrelevant because they are charged to other departments. (See Chapter 5 for a discussion of cost-effectiveness analysis.) Devolved budgeting through costcentres has been adopted by some institutions in order to give incentives to use 'owned resources'. You might like to consider the patterns of resource allocations within institutions and how they are changing. In researching these issues you might like to look again at the research suggestions discussed earlier in the chapter in relation to systems analysis and the open system model.

Resource allocations are a very effective means of control within an institution:

> Some institutions are reallocating key resources in ways which force change. The most common strategy is the reallocation of teaching space as learning space or learning resource centres so that it becomes impossible to book conventional teaching rooms for conventional teaching. (Gibbs *et al.*, 1994, p.11)

Not all institutions are changing their resourcing patterns in the same way, but this is a common pattern. You may already be experiencing changes along these lines, or may see them in the future. Such changes can be threatening, involving radical re-evaluations of the teaching role. Whether you see them as constructive or destructive, you will be in a much better position to understand, adapt if necessary, and defend your point of view, if you have an accurate idea of the resource implications for the institution of any changes in the delivery of your courses. A resource audit could be used to facilitate discussion within the organization and can optimize the use of existing resources. You will also have an idea of current costs to compare with the effects of any changes you might wish to make or be required to make because of institutional direction.

RESEARCH TASK. RESOURCE AUDIT

Calculate those resources available to support a particular course which you have direct control over. You will need to consider the following:

- academic staff time spent in class-contact activities such as lectures, seminars and other forms of supervised learning
- time spent in preparing for delivery and the development or identification of course materials, assessment and administration

---

- time spent in support activities such as counselling and individual remedial tutoring
- space allocations included in timetabled contact time (and perhaps your office)
- resources controlled directly by your department such as laboratory manuals, equipment and any locally held collections of materials
- costs of material production such as photocopied lecture handouts and course guides
- institutional overheads – administration, heating, etc.

Can you relate this investment to outcomes in terms of structured student learning time in hours? If this is not an appropriate measure, what would be better?

Ask each of the departmental managers responsible for providing learning resources in your institution to assist you in identifying resources available to you and your students. The more specific your request, the easier this will be. It is possible that resources are being acquired for a different course which would benefit your students. Are you regularly informed of new materials and services offered?

- ask the IT centre to give you an annotated list of computer programs relevant to your subject
- ask the library or resource centre to produce lists of materials
- find out what study space and computer facilities are available to your students for individual work. Are there areas where unsupervised group study work can take place? Are there any spaces currently under-utilized?
- find out what expertise is available to assist your students in learning resource departments or to assist you in curriculum development or resources production. You might like to consider other academic staff as well as support staff.

Determine whether resources are effectively exploited. Are there resources you are only now becoming aware of? Can students find material which could be useful? You might like to undertake a survey of student opinion which could reveal problem areas and potential improvements in support. How are they informed about resources and assisted to find them? Is there any scope for designing courses with awareness of what resource strengths exist, rather than designing a course and acquiring new resources to support it? Consider issues of security and student access (assistance available and opening hours) for material held in departments or in central facilities.

As a result of this audit, identify any areas where efficiency gains could be made with or without radical changes in your teaching strategy. Suggest improvements in resource exploitation which would be of interest to other practitioners.

Staff Development

Staff development is often identified as a key component of effective management of change. In considering how staff development activity can make change a constructive process you might like to consider the following research project.

Day *et al.* (1996) have reported on the Impel Project (Impact on People of Electronic Libraries) which 'has been investigating the human aspects of increased electronic library provision in academic libraries'. This looked at the impacts on library and information staff working in the higher education sector in the UK. Work was based on case studies. A questionnaire survey was used to select six sites for further sampling. Case studies adopted a triangulation approach: semi-structured, in-depth interviews, questionnaires and scrutiny of documentation. Findings were then validated and discussed at a participants' workshop which opened the way for future collaboration and for change monitoring. The study noted the following factors in success:

- Clarity of vision for the networked campus: the extent to which that vision is shared and understood by staff at all levels has a direct bearing on staff motivation.
- Exposition and implementation of strategy: translating the vision into practical, yet sensitive, strategic plans which recognize the problems of those who make strategies work is a fundamental requirement.
- Relations between groups: notably the interrelationships between library, computing, academic staff and students. Boundaries between these staff become blurred although interdependence increases. Close collaboration is important.
- Training and development: continuing and initial, helps staff to adapt more comfortably to change.
- Management structures: many library and information services retain traditional hierarchies although some are adopting teamwork approaches.
- Management of change: planning, training and good communications are needed to avoid fire-fighting and resentment or bewilderment among staff.

Institutions have adopted a variety of approaches to staff development. Some may expect staff to take most or all of the responsibility for their own professional development, sometimes it is coordinated within departments, others may provide central facilities to coordinate activity.

Many organizations have set up staff development units, in some cases closely integrated with centralized learning resources: for example, Thames Valley University has set up a 'University Centre for Complementary Learning' (Gibbs *et al.*, 1994) which is responsible for, among other things:

- providing and promoting continuing education activities across the university
- providing a focus for curriculum development and innovation
- providing a focus for research into teaching and learning
- providing a base for management and staff development programmes.

Smith (1993) describes an alternative model of a staff development programme at the University of Central England. Staff developers drawn from academic staff were reassigned on a part-time basis to serve each faculty, managing faculty resource centres and assisting academic staff with specific innovations in teaching and learning methods. Their brief was to promote the use of equipment and materials to enable staff to adapt to a changing educational context. They found that academic staff: 'made mixed use of the facilities of the Faculty Learning Centres; on average they were satisfied with them, but they consulted faculty staff developers very little' (Smith, 1993, p.102).

Results of surveys indicated that academic staff value activities such as workshops, seminars, regular dissemination of information, demonstrations of good practice, personal consultation over course planning, and evaluation of teaching and study skills courses for students, but had reservations about the status of the staff developer as an expert.

You might like to undertake a research task which focuses on the effectiveness of a new self-devised staff development programme. This would need to take account of your particular institutional context and the facilities, including your own time, available. It would be foolish to raise expectations which the institution is not able or willing to meet. You may like to adapt the following research task to a suitable scale. You could choose to look at more specific areas such as developments in teaching methods in relation to new or well-established educational technology, or the production of in-house teaching resources.

RESEARCH TASK. INVESTIGATING PROCEDURES FOR STAFF DEVELOPMENT IN RELATION TO RESOURCES

Undertake a survey based on a combination of semi-structured interviews of representative staff and a questionnaire sent to all staff in your institution – academic, support and administrative – which would provide information about current activities and provide an audit of staff needs to identify what form of support is felt appropriate and what untapped skill resources are available within the institution.

In a semi-structured interview with representative staff you could ask the following questions:

- What development activities have you been involved with in the last six months?
- Who was responsible for organizing the training?
- Have you organized any training activities?
- Was it done on a formal or informal basis?
- Please identify examples of good and bad aspects of the training.

In a questionnaire you could ask:

- What skills do you feel you need to develop? You could list the following as topic headings and ask for suggestions to be listed under each one:

    - IT skills including skills relating to the use of particular resources such as the Internet, CD-ROM and e-mail
    - skills relating to use of particular pieces of equipment
    - skills relating to teaching materials production
    - development of specific teaching skills
    - management skills
    - research and writing for publication skills.

- What skills do you have already which you feel you could share with others?
- Which of the following activities would you find or have you found constructive?

    - staff workshops (where information is pooled)
    - visits to other institutions
    - demonstrations and seminars (led by an 'expert')
    - drop-in sessions with staff identified as having particular skills to share
    - wider dissemination of information gathered by individuals, for example, routine circulation of notes taken at conferences.

Validate the information drawn from the interviews and the survey through a participant workshop with some of the respondents to discuss the findings.

A small working group could be formed at this workshop to take on the responsibility for organizing a pilot programme designed to address specified needs identified with resources available.

Monitor the effectiveness of the programme through consideration of:

- Numbers of staff attending events.
- Feedback from staff obtained through short standardized assessment forms.
- Any accounts gathered of new initiatives developed as a result of training sessions.
- Any accounts of the effect of these events on participants' subsequent working experiences.

Write up an evaluation of the effectiveness of the programme and relate the costs incurred (including the time of all the participants) to the benefits accrued. Identify the lessons learnt that you could share with others.

Cooperation between Institutions

Most of this chapter has dealt with ways in which institutions can optimize their own resources through internal cooperation. It would also be worth investigating ways in which cooperation between institutions can benefit the learning resources environment. Laurillard emphasizes this:

> It is inefficient to promote quality through competition because higher education has limited public resources to provide a public service... competition between institutions for resources for developing educational media creates a tremendous burden on staff... allows norm-referenced selection, ensures repetition of effort, encourages divisiveness.... (Laurillard, 1993, p. 224)

She is writing in the context of institutions producing resources for learning. We have already mentioned that some institutions have begun the production of their own resources. Gibbs *et al.* (1994) include several case studies in which institutions emphasize the production of in-house resources. The production of resources is very expensive and time-consuming and many institutions prefer to buy in resources when they can. There are a number of organizations which either coordinate the production and dissemination of resource materials or produce them themselves. Initiatives in the UK include the Computers in Teaching Initiative Centres and the Teaching and Learning Technology Programme. You might like to investigate the potential uses of resources

developed by these programmes or explore the possibility of cooperation with partners at other institutions in producing resources. Another phenomenon worth investigating is the potential of purchasing
consortia such as the Combined Higher Education Software Team
(CHEST) based in Bath which has negotiated price discounts for various
software licences and purchases for their members.

The Follett report suggested that, 'one approach to dealing with
pressures on space and stock might be sought in greater collaboration
and resource sharing between institutions' (Follett, 1993, p.42). It
suggests that cooperative acquisition strategies within a particular geo-
graphic area and giving 'users of collaborating institutions access to
each others' holdings' might be beneficial. Libraries have provided inter-
library loan facilities, coordinated by the British Library for many years.
You might like to explore the issue of 'access not holdings' in the context
of library provision and the extent to which an institution can afford to
acquire all that might possibly be useful to staff and students. You could
look at the development of short loan collections and focused study
packs to meet student needs.

Summary

In this chapter we have looked at different approaches to and examples
of the resources environment in its institutional context. We have made
suggestions for research enhancing cooperation and understanding in
a fluid situation. The next chapter will examine specific teaching issues
emerging from the resource environment.

Annotated Reading List

Gibbs, G, Pollard, N and Farrell, J (1994) *Institutional Support for Resource
Based Learning*, Oxford: The Oxford Centre for Staff Development,
Oxford Brookes University.
Includes a number of case studies focusing on the ways institutions have
implemented RBL.
Slowey, M (ed.) (1995) *Implementing Change from Within Universities and
Colleges*, London: Kogan Page.
Weil, S (ed.) (1994) *Introducing Change from the Top in Universities and Colleges*,
London: Kogan Page.
Both these books provide a collection of 'stories' or personal accounts of
the experiences of senior or middle managers in colleges and universities.

Underwood, P (1990) *Managing change in Libraries and Information Services: A systems approach,* London: Bingley.
An introduction to a variety of planning techniques within the context of a systems approach to resources management.

References

Anderson, G (1990) *Fundamentals of Educational Research,* London: Falmer Press.

Ashcroft, K, Bigger, S and Coates, D (1996) *Researching into Equal Opportunities in Colleges and Universities.* London: Kogan Page.

Bennett, C, Foreman-Peck, L and Higgins, C (1996) *Researching into Teaching Methods in Colleges and Universities,* London: Kogan Page.

Boyer, E L (1987) *College: The Undergraduate Experience in America,* New York: Harper and Row.

Brewer, J G (1988) *Guidelines for Learning Resources in Colleges,* Ely: Peter Francis.

Day, J M, Walton, G and Edwards, C (1996) 'The human face of change', *Library Technology,* 1, 1, 18.

Department for Education (DfE) (1993) *Higher Quality and Choice: The charter for higher education,* London: DfE.

Follett, B (Chairman) (1993) *Joint Funding Council's Libraries Review Group: Report,* Bristol: Higher Education Funding Council for England (HEFCE)

Gibbs, G, Pollard, N and Farrell, J (1994) *Institutional Support for Resource Based Learning,* Oxford: The Oxford Centre for Staff Development, Oxford Brookes University.

Laurillard, D (1993) *Rethinking University Teaching: A framework for the effective use of educational technology,* London and New York: Routledge.

Reekie, J (1990) Chapter 5 in Rust, C (ed.) *Changes of Course: Eight case studies of innovations in higher education courses,* Birmingham: Standing Conference on Educational Development.

Slowey, M (ed) (1995) *Implementing Change from within Universities and Colleges,* London: Kogan Page.

Smith, G (1993) 'Staff development by stealth', *British Journal of Educational Technology,* 24, 2, 102–13.

Underwood, P (1990) *Managing Change in Libraries and Information Services: A systems approach,* London: Bingley.

Weil, S (ed.) (1994) *Introducing Change from the Top in Universities and Colleges,* London: Kogan Page.

Yin, R K (1981) *Case Study Research: Design and methods,* Beverly Hills, CA: Sage.

Chapter 4

Resources and Teaching Issues

Introduction

In this chapter, we discuss ways of evaluating learning resources and researching their use. We explore in greater detail the theories of learning mentioned in Chapter 2 and introduce some other theoretical constructs that can be helpful when evaluating resources. We introduce these ideas in the context of the use of computer-assisted learning (CAL) materials and then discuss some more traditional resources. We then consider the roles of tutors and academic support staff and how teaching approaches can be developed to enhance the use of a range of learning resources.

Computer-Assisted Learning (CAL) Materials

There is a view of CAL as principally an instructional tool, but we should also consider its uses as a means of enhancing teaching and learning. One problem when considering research into CAL activities is the range of materials and modes of use that the term encompasses. The resources can vary from simple drill-and-practice programs to complex multimedia environments. The modes of use can range from a single student working alone with a rigid programmed learning sequence, to groups of students working with tutor intervention on a dynamic modelling activity. To make some sense of this complexity we need some organizing principles to help us as we research and evaluate.

Educational Paradigms

A useful frame of reference when considering CAL styles was developed during the evaluation phase of the UK National Development Programme in CAL. The evaluation team proposed four basic educational paradigms to distinguish the educational approach taken in a particular

CAL activity (for details see MacDonald *et al.*, 1977). The ideas proposed were very influential and have been adopted and adapted by later writers. We shall summarize briefly the four paradigms so that you can use the approach as a tool for characterizing CAL software (for a fuller discussion of these ideas see, for example, Sewell, 1990).

First is the *instructional* paradigm. This is associated with behavioural learning theory and is posited on the beliefs that the learning process can be rigorously analysed and that knowledge can be specified in language and transmitted to a student. An educational theory support-ing this view was outlined by Skinner (1953) in his doctrine of operant conditioning. Gagné's (1977) ideas on instructional design developed this notion. More recently, by incorporating learning theory from cognitive psychology, this has developed into instructional psychology, an overview of which can be found in Glaser (1987).

The essentials of the instructional paradigm can be summarized as follows (taken from MacDonald *et al.*, 1977, p. 38):

Key concept:	mastery of content
Curriculum emphasis:	subject matter as the object of learning
Educational means:	rationalization of instruction, especially in terms of sequencing presentation and feedback reinforcement
Role of the computer:	presentation of content, task prescription, student motivation through fast feedback
Assumptions:	conventional body of subject matter with articulated structure; articulated hierarchy of tasks; behaviouristic learning theory.

Second we have the *revelatory* paradigm. Here the emphasis is on the discovery by the student of the ideas in the field of study and the assumption that there is a knowledge structure which the student can master. Theorists from educational psychology that would be associated with this approach are Bruner (1966), with his ideas of the spiral curriculum, and Ausubel, with his concept of the advance organizer (1968).

The essentials of the revelatory paradigm can be summarized as follows (taken from MacDonald *et al.*, 1977, p.39):

Key concept:	discovery, intuition, getting a 'feel' for ideas in the field, etc
Curriculum emphasis:	the student as the subject of education
Educational means:	provision of opportunities for discovery and vicarious experience

Role of the computer: simulation or information-handling
Assumptions: (hidden) model of significant concepts and
                        knowledge structure; theory of learning by
                        discovery.

The third paradigm is the *conjectural* paradigm. This is associated with the constructivist learning theories of Piaget (1971) and, particularly in the context of information technology, the discussions of Papert (1980), which incorporate the view that knowledge is created through experience and evolves as a social process.

The essentials of the conjectural paradigm can be summarized as follows (taken from MacDonald et *al.*, 1977, p.40):

Key concept: articulation and manipulation of ideas and
                        hypothesis-testing
Curriculum emphasis: understanding, 'active' knowledge
Educational means: manipulation of student inputs, finding
                        metaphors and model building
Role of the computer: manipulable space/field/'scratch-pad'/
                        language, for creating or articulating models,
                        programs, plans or conceptual structures
Assumptions: problem-oriented theory of knowledge;
                        general cognitive theory.

These three paradigms are all firmly rooted in educational theories of learning. However, when used outside education, perhaps the most powerful argument for computer use is that it saves labour. To incorporate this additional element, MacDonald et *al.* (1977) introduce a possible fourth paradigm to consider when evaluating approaches to CAL material by using the idea of 'authentic' labour. They suggest that we can think of student activity as labour and they distinguish between 'authentic' labour (valued learning) and 'inauthentic' labour (activities which may be instrumental to valued learning, but which are not valued for their own sake). Under this analysis, CAL applications which can be categorized by the first three paradigms can all be thought of as enhancing authentic student labour. However, many CAL applications improve the learning experience by making certain tasks easier or less tedious; for example large amounts of information can be handled faster using a database; or complex calculations can be carried out with little effort using a spreadsheet or statistical package. The paradigm they introduce to cover those activities that reduce inauthentic labour is called the *emancipatory* paradigm, which can appear in association with one of the other three. The benefit of CAL applications that incorporate elements of this paradigm is that the emancipatory role allows students to devote more time to the more valuable authentic labour of the original paradigm.

You can use these four paradigms to make a start on the task of sorting out what types of CAL software you have available to you, and then begin to consider the forms of CAL activity to which each is suited, as each style can require a different mode of use.

RESEARCH TASK. CATEGORIZING CAL SOFTWARE

Discover who keeps lists of software available in your institution. They may be held by the library, the resources centre, the computer centre, subject departments, etc.

Select some software relevant for your discipline to review. Attempt to categorize each piece of software by the educational approaches employed as suggested by the paradigms. For example:

- obvious drill-and-practice programs are instructional;
- even the more sophisticated tutorial-style software is still predominantly instructional in our terms;
- simulations are essentially revelatory, as the emphasis is on discovering how the implied model works by varying inputs and observing effects;
- adventure games can be thought of as fantasy simulations and so in that sense are revelatory, though some may have elements of the conjectural paradigm;
- so called 'microworlds' such as LOGO, which provide an environment for the student to manipulate, are conjectural;
- word-processors, databases, spreadsheets and information CD-ROMs are emancipatory.

Use a variety of these programmes with your students. Get them to evaluate which they found:

- enjoyable;
- useful in the context of their learning;
- easy or frustrating to use;
- demanding and/or challenging.

Use your data as the basis for a paper discussing the student response to programs within each paradigm and the potential and limitations such paradigms impose or create.

Self-study Tutorials

Having considered the software available to you, you may decide that there is nothing particular to your needs and that you want to create your own customized packages. It might be fruitful to develop a CAL self-study tutorial that dealt with subject knowledge that was either a prerequisite for a course or basic content covered during a course. Students could work through such a tutorial at their own pace and in their own time, checking which course topics they understood, and concentrating on any individual weak areas that they discovered.

Elements of the behaviourist approach of the first paradigm can be identified in many such tutorial programs. This theory focuses attention on what the student does and the responses they give. Its simplest form, the Skinner approach, was exemplified in the early teaching machines. Here some new material was presented to the student; a response was called for, for example a question was posed or a missing space had to be filled in; reinforcing feedback was then given when the response was correct, and the program moved on. These crude teaching machines were not generally popular. However, the ideas have been developed and now programs that have some behaviourist elements offer feedback on both correct and incorrect responses, giving information to help the user identify errors and correct them. This implies that the programs have a branching structure to allow students to follow individual paths through the program, depending on their responses.

You can develop this sort of tutorial using an authoring package. In its simplest form an authoring package essentially allows you to create a program which, when used by a student, presents pages or 'frames' of text in an order determined by the user's responses. For example, a frame with some information will be presented to a student who can then choose from a selection of what to see next, or a frame with a question will be presented and the student chooses from a list of possible answers. The program then presents the next frame depending on the response – perhaps more information, or confirmation of a correct response, or some attempt to diagnose the error after an incorrect response – and the process repeats. Merrill (1985) discusses features which authoring systems should have and considers the advantages and disadvantages of their use.

To develop such a self-study tutorial you might concentrate on the concepts involved rather than the procedures used. As Laurillard concludes after a survey of research studies of what students bring to learning: 'what students know can be described in a relatively concise way, as long as you penetrate to the level of what the concept means to the student' (Laurillard, 1993, p.37). She goes on to give a striking example of two studies to do with subtraction. One study of subtraction procedures found 89 ways of doing it incorrectly, whereas another found just two ways of misconceptualizing subtraction.

RESEARCH TASK. DEVELOPING A CAL SELF-STUDY TUTORIAL

Decide what knowledge and concepts are required or developed in the part of the course you are considering.

Ask a cohort of students which basic concepts they had trouble under-standing. You could use a semi-structured interview technique to discover the main areas in which they had misconceptions, and then prompt for any other areas you thought they had not considered or were not aware of (for details of a semi-structured interview schedule, see Bennett et al., 1996). Areas you might investigate could include:

- What technical terms have everyday meaning that could lead to their misinterpretation?
- What kinds of naive conceptions might be prevalent in this topic?
- Which forms of representation (linguistic, notational, diagrammatic, graphical, symbolic, iconic, numeric) are difficult to handle?

You will now have a body of material that might be included in a tutorial. Attempt to organize it into a structured body with a hierarchy of knowledge and concepts as suggested by the paradigm.

Use an authoring package to develop a tutorial that will take a student through the body of material, explaining the concepts and testing their understanding of it.

Use a variety of evaluation techniques (see Ashcroft and Palacio, 1996, for details) to explore the effectiveness of this model of CAL, compared with more traditional methods of teaching the same concepts. Use your results as the starting point for a discursive paper about the shortcomings and benefits of CAL, based on a model of hierarchical knowledge.

Theories of Learning and their Effect on CAL in Use

Having gone some way to developing a tool for categorizing software styles, another approach would be to carry out some research into CAL material in use, in an attempt to determine the educational value of CAL activities based on various models of learning.

As any piece of CAL software incorporates more or less explicitly the model of learning its designer espouses, the educational value of CAL should be considered relative to this theoretical model. Different models will have different aims and objectives for the learning process and will require varying modes of use. You will need to delve into these theories of learning and to consider different ways of assessing and evaluating the educational processes and learning outcomes involved.

Two broad categories of CAL software can be identified in terms of the learning theory models used for their design. The first category comprises that software where the designer takes a behaviourist view of learning, and the second is where the programs are modelled on cognitive theories of learning.

Behaviourist Approaches

This category includes software within the instructional paradigm characterization of our previous discussion. This is a very popular mode as it is, perhaps at least superficially, the easiest to create. The problem is that it is also easy to create bad instructional software. Instructional software can, however, be shown to be effective in certain specific learning situations. An approach you might take to explore such a claim would be that of meta-analysis.

Meta-analysis is a research technique that enables a large number of diverse research studies of a topic to be reviewed, with the aim of obtaining an overview of general trends. Advocated by Glass (1976), it allows the results of a large number of studies to be integrated by statistical analysis. A report of the results of over 100 meta-analytic studies in education can be seen in Kulik and Kulik (1989). Useful discussions of the methodology are contained in Glass *et al.* (1981) and Wolf (1986).

To give a flavour of the approach, we shall consider one of the techniques employed. This uses the notion of a measure of the 'effect size' of the results reported in a particular study. Size of effect can be measured in different ways but the most often used (Glass' effect size) is calculated by taking the difference between the average scores of the experimental and control groups and dividing by the standard deviation of the measure employed. This gives a standardized index of the difference in outcomes for the experimental and control groups of the study. The effect sizes from a variety of studies can then be expressed on a common scale and further statistical analysis carried out.

An example of the techniques applied in the realm of computer-based instruction can be found in Kulik (1994). This gives a review of findings of a number of meta-analytic studies, and also includes an analysis of 97 studies of school use of CAL. The results include such findings as: computer tutoring programs, including drill-and-practice or tutorials (ie our category of instructional programs), have a positive effect on student learning; students learn better in courses that include some computer tutoring; and computer tutoring compares favourably with other innovations, particularly for average students.

Thus in certain learning situations instructional programs appear to be successful in terms of the aims and objectives of the teaching and learning process of these situations. Such a situation for a drill-and-practice program might be where a certain skill or some material has to be 'over-learned' so that it can be carried out or recalled automatically at some higher level of activity (see Gagné, 1982 for a discussion of what he calls 'automaticity'). For example, in mathematics the basic algebraic skills of manipulation of expressions, rearrangement of terms, factorization of equations and so on are a prerequisite for the effective solution of problems and discernment of patterns in higher algebra. The lack of these basic skills as an automatic part of the mathematician's repertoire can hinder or even prevent the successful solution of a problem.

You might also evaluate the effectiveness of a particular piece of instructional CAL software. There are two areas you could investigate: the outcomes of the activity and the actual process of carrying it out. To investigate the outcomes, you will need to determine the objectives of the program. To investigate the process, you need to be aware of the mode of use. Knowing both of these elements will influence what you decide to evaluate and how you can evaluate it.

First, the objectives: instructional software may essentially be concerned with the delivery of subject matter. The drill-and-practice end of the spectrum is about learning content and mastering simple techniques, while the tutorial end encompasses a more complex view of learning as a hierarchy of knowledge through which the learner progresses, by moving from simple ideas and skills up to more complex ideas and skills.

Second, the mode of use: working with an instructional program is normally a solitary business and the processes of data gathering about this facet of the activity must reflect this. Observation of the activity will not necessarily enable you to discover what is happening.

RESEARCH TASK. EVALUATION OF
INSTRUCTIONAL CAL – 'THINK ALOUD' PROTOCOL

You can investigate both the outcomes of the activity and the actual process of carrying it out.

Outcomes:
- Decide what the objectives of the program are, for example in terms of:

  - the content to be covered;
  - the concepts to be developed;
  - the skills to be practised, etc.

- Decide how you will measure the progress of the students:

  - Will you carry out pre- and post-tests of the students using the program?
  - Will you have a control group using traditional methods of instruction and an experimental group using the software to compare them with?

- Decide on measures of success in meeting objectives.

Process:
- Decide what information you want to know about the process, for example:

  - Is it easy for the user to see what to do at any stage?
  - Are there any unclear or ambiguous passages?
  - Are any examples used clear and effective?
  - Is the feedback to the user's responses helpful and appropriate?

- Decide how you will gather information about the process of the activity:

  - some of the information you require can be gathered by using questionnaires or interviews; these will obviously gather data after the event;
  - an interesting technique for gathering data as the activity develops is the 'think aloud' protocol.

Think aloud protocol. With this technique, the student says whatever comes into their head as they carry out the activity. This can be captured verbatim with a tape recorder or an observer can make notes. The comments can then be analysed and categorized.

The approach is open-ended and undirected and can gather data which are unavailable using other methods. It allows some insight into the thought processes of the student as they work.

> One problem with the method is that sometimes the student will fall silent just as things get interesting, simply because their thought processes are becoming too complex to voice. A way round this problem is to let the student complete the task undisturbed and then to ask them to complete a reflective, retrospective account of how they carried out the activity.

For further information on the theory of instructional design, see Gagné (1975; 1977), Gagné and Briggs (1979) and Reigeluth (1983); and particularly with reference to CAL, see Jonassen (1988) and Gagné (1982).

Cognitive Theories

The second category of CAL software consists of those programs which are modelled on cognitive theories of learning. In contrast to the behaviourist approach where the student is considered to be a passive recipient of teaching, the cognitive theories consider the student as an active participant in the learning process, which process is seen as the development and modification of cognitive structures.

One of the most influential theorists in this field has been Jean Piaget (1971). He propounded the view that knowledge could be structured and organized by means of 'schemata' which can be thought of as abstract representations of concepts (an idea originally developed in the pioneering work of Bartlett, 1932). The structure is developed and modified by the processes of 'assimilation', 'accommodation' and 'equilibration'. Assimilation involves taking in new information to the existing structure. Accommodation describes the modification of schemata to cope with this new material. This modification is necessary, he suggested, because subjects wish to maintain an equilibrium in their cognitive systems between their experience and their cognitive structures, thus carrying out the process of equilibration. The other important element of the theory that he proposed was that the systematic changes which occur as a result of equilibration cause the knowledge structure to change in discernible stages, which appear in a fixed order.

The emphasis of this approach is on the internal processing of ideas, and is termed 'constructivist' theory as the learner constructs their own understanding. For fuller details of these complex ideas, see Piaget's own writings or a commentary on them by, for example, Flavell (1963) or Brown and Desforges (1979).

The prime example of CAL software to incorporate these ideas is LOGO, the programming language for geometry, one of whose main designers, Seymour Papert, worked for a time with Piaget. Papert's book *Mindstorms* (1980), discusses how computers could be used for education by utilizing the approach of constructing 'microworlds', that is computer environments for students to test ideas and hypotheses about the knowledge structure under consideration.

These ideas conflate two of the paradigms of our earlier discussion – the revelatory and the conjectural. The essential difference is that in revelatory software the emphasis is on a body of knowledge in a hidden knowledge structure being revealed to the student by exploration and discovery, whereas in conjectural software the emphasis is more on the development of the cognitive activities involved in the discovery, for example the development of problem-solving skills, hypothesis-testing skills and procedural thinking skills. Claims are made that these constructivist microworlds can develop transferable cross-curricular skills. A possible area of research would be to investigate whether there is any transfer of skills from one knowledge domain to another. For an excellent review of research in this area, see Perkins and Salomon (1989).

These original constructivist ideas take little account of the social context of the learning process. The implication is that individual exploration of the learning environment and operations which in some way embody the knowledge or principles involved, will result in assimilation and accommodation of the new knowledge into existing schemata with a concomitant development of the student's knowledge structures. Later developments in cognitive theory do not treat learning as a solitary, individualistic activity but rather attempt to incorporate the effects of the student's peers and the teaching process involved.

One of the primary influences for development of this view is the work of the Russian psychologist, Lev Vygotsky, whose writings did not start to appear in the West until almost 30 years after his death in 1934. They are now the basis of much of this new development which is commonly termed 'socio-cultural theory' (see Bruner, 1985; Newman *et al.*, 1989; Wertsch, 1985). One of the main propositions of his work is the concept of the 'zone of proximal development', defined as:

> the distance between the actual development level as determined by independent problem solving and the level of potential development as determined through problem solving under adult guidance or in collaboration with more capable peers. (Vygotsky, 1978, p.86)

The zone of proximal development thus refers to the area of cognitive ability that covers tasks beyond what a student can accomplish unaided, but which the student can complete with some support or prompting. The idea is that some form of guidance and structure of activities (in the original definition, from a teacher or the student's peers; in our context, from a computer program as well) can help to develop cognitive structures more effectively than random exploration would. Thus, the original notion of discovery learning in our revelatory paradigm has developed into guided discovery learning.

As Bruner, one of the major exponents of these ideas, says:

> Some years ago I wrote some very insistent articles about the importance of discovery learning – learning on one's own, or as Piaget put it later (and I think better), learning by inventing. What I am proposing here is an extension of that idea, or better a completion. My model of the child in those days was very much in the tradition of the solo child mastering the world by representing it to himself in his own terms. In the intervening years I have come increasingly to recognize that most learning in most settings is a communal activity, a sharing of the culture. It is not just that the child must make his own knowledge his own, but that he must make it his own in a community of those who share his sense of belonging to a culture. It is this that leads me to emphasize not only discovery and invention but the importance of negotiating and sharing. (Bruner, 1986, p.127)

If we characterize the educational theories discussed so far as Jones and Mercer (1993) do, then behaviourism can be seen as a theory of teaching, constructivism can be seen as a theory of learning, and socio-cultural theory can be seen as a theory of teaching-and-learning.

These cognitive theories were originally developed in the context of children's learning, but a similar analysis can be made of the nature of academic learning carried out by students at college and university level (see, for example, Laurillard, 1993 or Ramsden, 1992). The traditional view has been of knowledge as subject matter that could be presented by means of lectures and textbooks – the transmission model of the behaviourist theories. However, most lecturers are aware that purely imparting knowledge is unsuccessful as a teaching aim. Many students are unable to apply their existing knowledge in unfamiliar settings, to transfer knowledge from one area to another, or to relate theory to practice. This leads to the conclusion that their knowledge is context-related and to the ideas of 'situated learning' (see Brown *et al.*, 1989). An example of situated cognition is the well-established practice of exploring concrete examples of an idea or process before constructing an abstraction. In the end, academic knowledge has to be abstracted and represented formally, so that it can be generalized, reflected upon and applied most widely. Academic learning should be an activity that develops abstractions from multiple contexts – echoes of the constructivist theories we have been discussing. However, this is not the whole story. Academic learning is about how a subject is known as well as what is known. It is not only developed by experience but also by reflection on that experience. This is where the Vygotskyian elements of learning as a social process can come into play.

The implication of these ideas for the evaluation of CAL materials designed for use with cognitive theories of learning in mind, is that observational research techniques may be required, especially as the objectives are not purely to do with the transmission of subject matter to the students, but are also concerned with the interactions between the participants: students, tutor and CAL materials. A suggested technique for carrying out such an analysis is a form of discourse analysis.

RESEARCH TASK. DISCOURSE ANALYSIS

Gather as much data as you can about what takes place when students and the tutor use the CAL materials. You could:

- videotape the session;
- have observers watch the session and complete observation schedules;
- interview the participants;
- record a navigation trace of how the program was used (if the program has this facility);
- collect print-outs giving information on the state of the program;
- take copies of screen displays.

You can then carry out a detailed qualitative study of what happened during the session. Use this to evaluate the nature and quality of the educational processes that took place.
Introduce a form of discourse analysis:

- take a transcript of what was said;
- break it down into small units;
- relate to these units the interactions that took place, the participants' views of why they did whatever they did, and the screen displays and outputs as representations of the state of the program.

For further discussion of this technique, see Mercer (1990) or Tesch (1990), where what we are discussing comes under the headings of 'discourse analysis' and 'ethnography of communication'.

It is probably true that the majority of existing uses of CAL software fit the instructional paradigm. However, many theorists would predict that in the future the most effective uses of CAL will adopt cognitive approaches, that fit better with the way psychologists now think that cognition develops. However, the implication is that the CAL materials will have to be embedded in powerful learning environments. For a discussion of the design of such environments and the relative roles different learning resources might play in them, see Chapter 6.

Learning Styles and Learning Strategies

Another way of looking at CAL materials, and indeed all learning resources, is to consider the effects of different student learning styles and learning strategies on the material's use and effectiveness.

Various definitions of cognitive style or learning style have been made (see, for example, Kogan, 1971 or Messick, 1984) but in simple terms it can be thought of as a tendency to adopt certain strategies or methods when learning. Cognitive style can be seen as a significant personal characteristic which helps us to understand how people learn, but the point should be made that it is unlikely that a student can be neatly categorized as having a particular learning style at all times in all situations. There is evidence that learning strategies may be influenced by many factors, such as motivation, style of assessment, and so on (Marton and Säljö, 1976). Students may exhibit a mix of strategies in varying degrees in various situations, but it is argued that they will be influenced by their underlying style, and so the generalization of personal style does have some value.

Many different aspects of learning style have been reported (Kolb, 1984; Messick, 1970; Pask and Scott, 1972; Witkin, 1976) but Clarke suggests:

> The vast majority of cognitive styles can be classified into a preference for a reasonable degree of structure and guidance to be provided in the learning situation, or a preference for considerable freedom to choose the direction that learning should take. (Clarke, 1993, p.48)

He argues that these are the two extremes of a continuum of learning styles onto which most others can be placed.

Learning styles are manifested in learning strategies or the actual methods used to learn. Pask's experiments (Pask, 1976; Pask and Scott, 1972) identified learning strategies which corresponded to the styles at the extremes of the continuum. One strategy was termed 'serialist', indicating a preference for a step-by-step approach moving from one simple hypothesis to the next. The other strategy was termed 'holist', indicating a more global approach using more complex hypotheses concerning several properties at the same time. For a clear, well-written overview of this research, see Entwistle (1981).

We can describe serialists as preferring their information in well-defined separate topics, sequenced with simple links. They concentrate on the detail and form an overall picture later rather than sooner in the process. Holists have a wide focus of attention, look further ahead, look for links and try to build a broad overview early as a guide for their learning, and see where the details fit in at a later stage. Serialists would find anecdote, analogy and illustration distracting whereas holists would make much use of them. However, it must be said that both types of student can reach the same level of understanding: though they will get there by different routes.

Pask's experiments artificially accentuated differences in learning strategies to facilitate the study of them, but he argues that they are representative of discernible general learning styles. In normal learning situations he identifies students who act 'like holists' with the 'comprehension learning' style, which involves building a description of what is known and developing an overview of how topics are related. Students who act 'like serialists' he identifies with the 'operation learning' style, which involves mastering procedural details supporting the overview. Students who can act effectively in either way, depending on the task, are said to be 'versatile'. He emphasized that the comprehension/operation distinction is a matter of degree, but one that may be important because description-building and procedure-building operations may each be a prerequisite for understanding any topic.

Much work has gone into developing methods for determining learning styles: tests for field dependence-independence (Witkin *et al.*, 1977); Kolb's Learning Style Inventory (Kolb, 1984); Pask's procedures for identifying comprehension-operation styles (Pask, 1973; 1976). Many of these measures are lengthy and complex.

Building on Pask's work, Entwistle (1981) developed a 30-item questionnaire, the Short Inventory of Approaches to Studying, to identify comprehension, operation and versatile learning styles amongst other factors relating to learning. In turn, Ford (1985) developed an 18-item questionnaire, the Study Preference Questionnaire (SPQ), which was designed to assess preference for global description-building before local procedure-building, or vice-versa. The questionnaire is in the form of items to be rated on a Likert scale (see Bennett *et al.*, 1996 for a description of this). In a comparison of the items designed to assess comprehension or operation learning on the Short Inventory of

Approaches to Studying, and the items designed to assess holist or serialist preferences on the SPQ, he found four items which accurately predicted holist or serialist bias.

In another study, Clarke (1993) took the analysis a stage further and reduced the SPQ to a 13-item test which he claimed is more reliable than the original. Indeed, he then went on to identify the following single item which he suggested could perhaps be used to assess holist or serialist tendencies. An answer of '1' to the following question suggests a holist tendency and an answer of '5' suggests a serialist one:

| When I'm reading a book (or other information source) for my studies, I prefer to spend quite a long time skimming over and dipping into it to get a clear picture of what it's about and how it will be relevant. | 1 2 3 4 5 | When I'm reading a book (or other information source) for my studies, I prefer to get quite soon into a fairly detailed reading of it once I know that it's going to be useful, in the knowledge that its precise relevance and contribution will become clear from a detailed reading. |

where: 1 = I agree with the statement on the left.
2 = I agree (with reservations) with the statement on the left.
3 = No preference for either statement.
4 = I agree (with reservations) with the statement on the right.
5 = I agree with the statement on the right.

The point of this classification is that it has been found that matching or mismatching teaching strategies and materials with students' preferred learning strategies can enhance or inhibit effective learning (Ford, 1985; Pask, 1976). To investigate this yourself you could prepare different versions of teaching materials or explore different modes of use of CAL materials.

RESEARCH TASK. LEARNING STRATEGY INVESTIGATION

Choose a CAL package with potential for various modes of use, for example a CD-ROM information base.

Decide on some specific objectives you would like students to achieve by using this material:

- some information to discover;
- some concepts to learn;
- some skills to develop.

Develop some teaching materials to accompany the CAL package that match the serialist and holist learning strategies:

- for a serialist approach you could develop a guided tour of various elements, thus organizing a linear path through a sequence of experiences and information;
- for a holist approach you could prepare an overview or navigation map of the structure, together with some suggested lines of enquiry.

Use the single Clarke question with a group of students to assess broadly their personal learning strategies.

Investigate whether matching or mismatching personal strategy and material inhibits or enhances learning.

Traditional Learning Resource Activities

We now consider some more traditional resources and associated research tasks, and place them into the context of the learning theories we have introduced.

RESEARCH TASK. READING LIST

Hand out your usual reading list to your class of students with an assessment sheet questionnaire. This might take the following form of a record sheet to be completed by the student after reading any of the books:

- title of the book and reason for use;
- readability, eg, level of difficulty, language use;
- usefulness of the book as a source for the student's purpose;
- annotated notes of its key points/arguments;
- recommendation of its value on the reading list.

Collect and collate the responses. Use them to give you an insight into the value of your list as the students perceive it. You could use the information to modify the list, inform next year's students and/or write up the findings, analysing required and recommended course books. You could investigate whether a particular format of the questionnaire (for example, open-ended or more closed questions) yields the most useful information and whether it would be best to let students devise the questionnaire.

This task is active and involves practice within a given directed context, with reinforcement of the activity included. It thus fits a behaviourist perspective, but it also involves acquiring new knowledge, logically structuring work and giving learners information on their progress, and so it is possible to analyse it in terms of cognitive theory.

RESEARCH TASK. LABORATORY

Observe your students in a laboratory setting. Divide your class into groups.

Set a task which requires each group to use the materials in the laboratory in a specific way to complete the task.

Ensure that the groups will need to share equipment and laboratory space to complete the task within a set time.

Study the process by which students make or do not make the best use of the facilities to hand.

Use this study as the basis for a paper that speculates on the laboratory as a learning resource and your students' abilities to maximize its effectiveness.

Concentrate on their ability to perceive and make use of the laboratory as a resource in itself. Assess:

- whether they make best use of its special dimensions;
- whether they are familiar with what is available to use in their experiments in the laboratory itself;
- whether the equipment is selected, handled and dispensed effectively;
- how far the laboratory is perceived by students as a fixed asset not worthy of real consideration;
- how effectively tasks are undertaken within its confines.

In the task above learners are obliged to mesh old knowledge and approaches with new and develop effective sequencing of activities which lends itself to analysis in terms of cognitive theory, but they also work in a group atmosphere and take responsibility for their actions, which exemplifies socio-cultural theory.

RESEARCH TASK. PROJECT-BASED WORK

Students often collect and collate a variety of evidence from outside their institution of learning. In a number of instances this information remains unknown to you. In order to knit your students' random and uncoordinated sources together and to seek to ascertain their overall value, ask your students in groups to keep field notes of information gathered from outside the usual and expected communication channels of their course, for instance from conversations, visits to buildings, displays, exhibitions and conferences. Collate and record them in a systematic way, such as by:

- type of 'extra-curricular' resource;
- location of resource;
- value of the resource.

Ask the students to hand in a dossier, file or portfolio of field notes (preferably annotated) and collectively analyse their value. Discuss methods of expanding the information as a learning resource base for others, such as through having the groups collate the material into a project for wider use.

Having completed the project, individually interview each member of the group and see what use they made of varied resources, either formally or informally. Conduct a group interview about their response to a checklist of resources used, ensuring all have an opportunity to speak. Record the responses and use the discussion to analyse whether similar comments are emerging about the variety and use of what was available.

This kind of activity builds on learners' natural curiosity, can increase motivation, has a relevance built in and as such builds on socio-cultural theory ideas.

RESEARCH TASK. LECTURE/VISITING SPEAKER

There is scope for researching your lectures and those of visiting speakers in terms of their value as resources. Collect data in the following way:

- tape or video the lectures;
- ask another lecturer to carry out a written evaluation of the lecture.

Have a questionnaire completed individually and in confidence by the students who attended the lectures, asking questions such as:

- What did you like/dislike about the presentation?
- What did you learn and how well did you assimilate the information?
- To what extent can the results of the lecture be used as a learning resource?
- What was it like to be able to ask questions of a 'resource'?

(See Ashcroft and Palacio, 1996, for details of a variety of evaluation techniques.) Use the evaluation and student views to inform your perceptions of what took place.

Tasks like this help determine how far students are becoming responsible for their learning through having them question and consider relevance of particular approaches in a socio-cultural context.

Tutoring and Resources

Tutors and their supporting personnel, rather than CAL or traditional resources, are the prime learning resource. Ideally tutors are flexible, creative, adaptable and able to use other resources to meet their students' needs. Johnson and Samways (1993) stated that teachers should only be teachers if they themselves like to learn. However, there is a view that 'scholars utilize library collections remarkably little, the bibliographic apparatus even less, and librarians' reference services hardly at all' (Smith, 1990, p.21). It has been said that, 'The potential of technology is not widely understood among academic staff, and there is a clear need to develop and disseminate good practice' (NOAL, 1993, p.52). This is where the divide between tutors and academic support staff is increasingly becoming irrelevant. Collaboration and cooperation in the provision of effective teaching and learning strategies using greater resource provision, requires closer working together than ever before to enable a proactive resource centre to emerge.

Flexible learning necessitates wide use of expertise and skills. The library staff are potentially far more than a link between scholar and student. However, there may be uncertainty and doubt about how teaching and other staff should best work together to enhance student learning. The increasingly large number of students in further and higher education calls for the development of their research skills. This implies a need to collaborate to assist this development.

The traditional approach in higher education to students' learning has been to provide a series of lectures, seminars or tutorials and a reading list which suggests further sources of information. Students are expected to produce regular essays, contribute to seminar discussions and at the year or course end to taken written examinations to establish their grasp of knowledge, understanding and skills. There are problems with this model. Increasing student numbers may make the system unworkable. For instance, in the UK, lecture groups become so large that interaction through questioning is inhibited. Sometimes, seminar and tutorial groups are also too large for any real discussion between tutor and individual students in the group. Marking of assignments becomes a problem and library resources may be strained because of pressure of demand for books. As the ability range of students increases, the traditional transmission approach may become an increasingly inappropriate method for enhancing student learning.

Resource-based learning (RBL) is an alternative to traditional teaching approaches. RBL is not a bolt-on to existing courses or a hyped-up approach to existing resource use. It needs full support and to be built into teaching and course development time. Training in course design for implementing RBL effectively is important. To deliver RBL there should be academic staff working with library support staff who actually know the aims and objectives. A map through the process to the end product and the development of a network for exchanging information may help to prevent overlaps of material.

RESEARCH TASK. ACTION PLAN FRAMEWORK

Consider the possibilities of joining or setting up a network for exchanging ideas in your field of research. Develop an e-mail contact with a colleague in another learning institution. Discuss how you can both create a task for your respective students which requires use of e-mail to transmit appropriate information. (The nature, timing and expectation of the task need to be made explicit to your own groups of students.)

You may find creating a joint action plan framework (APF) helpful in identifying your aims with regard to student learning objectives. Questions you might jointly consider include:

- What are the aims of the task?
- What are the learning objectives to be achieved?
- What are the tasks to be undertaken?
- How does the content allow the end product to be achieved?
- Will a competency format be used?
- How will assessment be achieved?
- Can you devise an APF grid to encapsulate what you want to achieve?
- How does the librarian fit into this process in terms of aims, objectives, content, methodology, activities and ultimately evaluation?

Following the task evaluate how far the students were able to cope with the exercise, its success in achieving the aims and learning objectives, and the possibilities and pitfalls in developing such a mode of contact as a specific learning resource.

If the student-centred approach leads to resources simply being seen as the materials and technology to deliver what is required, then the process of full educational development of the student may be left out of the learning resource context. Open learning can facilitate student-centred work but planning must encompass course development, the production of learning materials and their effective delivery. These are concerns that need to be shared between tutor, academic support staff and student. Certainly 'open learning won't work unless learners learn how to learn' (Cunningham, in Hodgson *et al.*, 1987, p.40).

Integrated learning resource provision may be the best way forward in an increasingly multimedia and interdisciplinary context. Having tutors 'dabbling' with resources and support staff 'dabbling' with teaching may not be the answer. Without integrated planning, there is a danger of hastily and ill-prepared pre-packaged material being produced by a variety of facilitators of learning in the institution. A pathway through the forest of information may result from the consultative process, as well as open learning packages that include a look at objectives, activities, style and exemplars (Lewis and Paine, 1986).

There is likely to be an improvement in the effective use of resources where librarians work in partnership with teaching staff to develop information skills in library users. Induction sessions are important in this. There is also scope for making good use of students' life skills and knowledge, such as of computer software and applications, which they can 'transmit' to fellow students in structured sessions.

Wengraf (1995) discusses the possibilities of 'empowering undergraduate students as action researchers into student learning'. He writes:

> I argue that undergraduate students are professional learners who need *institutionalized* support from academic staff to enable them to be 'professionally reflective' (Schon, 1987) about their practice as students... [because]... staff's *informal* grasp of the conditions of student learning can no longer be relied upon to substitute for student self-knowledge achieved through institutionally supported and required collective self-research. One way of doing this is to *institutionalize undergraduate action research as part of ordinary coursework.*
> (Wengraf, 1995, p.165; emphasis in the original)

He describes a project in which first-year students on a human sciences research methods module were asked to do semi-structured interviews for a coursework report on the topic 'What could be done to improve module X?' The students learnt research techniques, demonstrated high motivation and application, and provided useful data in evaluating the course. You might like to investigate ways in which students can participate in research designed to discover more effective ways of addressing their needs. You might use research of this kind to help the students find ways of developing their capacity to learn through understanding the processes they are engaged in.

The more actively a student has to process information the more likely they are to retain it and be able to use that information constructively and flexibly. Harel and Papert (1992) give a fascinating account of research in one very active learning environment. A fourth-grade class in Boston was engaged for a semester in the design and production of educational software to teach fractions to younger children. The children not only understood fractions much better at the end of the project and learnt sophisticated programming techniques but, most importantly, became personally engaged with the process of learning as they explored the ways younger children learnt from their programs. They showed significant improvements in problem-solving ability and motivation. In this example, the resources available to the students were computers and a programming software package, the communication between each other and with teachers and their own imagination. This research raised many interesting issues about the effect that instructing others has on one's own understanding of a subject.

RESEARCH TASK. DESIGNING A RESOURCE

Ask your students to design a resource such as a display or an audio-visual presentation, with supporting materials, which other students can use to learn about a subject on your course.

Use a questionnaire to test the comprehension of the material of those who designed the resource, those who used the resource, and a control group taught in a conventional way.

Summary

In this chapter we have discussed the theoretical frameworks for considering the use of resources in the teaching and learning context, taking CAL as an exemplar. We have also considered how these approaches could be applied to more traditional resources. The next chapter will consider more specific needs of individual students.

Annotated Reading List

Entwistle, N J (1981) Styles of Learning and Teaching: An integrated outline of educational psychology for students, teachers and lecturers, New York: John Wiley.
A lucid introduction to educational psychology for those with little previous knowledge of the subject, with the emphasis placed on learning in higher education.

Hodgson, V E, Mann, S J and Snell, R S (eds) (1987) *Beyond Distance Teaching – Towards Open Learning*, Buckingham: Open University Press.
Useful for looking at the role of learning resources in the area of knowledge and at the link between resources and the Kolb Learning Cycle.
Sewell, D (1990) *New Tools for New Minds*, Brighton: Harvester Wheatsheaf.
A cognitive perspective on the use of computers, written by a psychologist. Although essentially about the use of computers with children it is a very readable account of many of the ideas discussed in this chapter.

References

Ashcroft, K and Palacio, D (1996) *Researching into Evaluation and Assessment in Colleges and Universities*, London: Kogan Page.
Ausubel, D P (1968) *Educational Psychology: A cognitive view*, New York: Holt, Rhinehart and Winston.
Bartlett, F C (1932) *Remembering: A study in experimental and social psychology*, Cambridge: Cambridge University Press.
Bennett, C, Foreman-Peck, L and Higgins, C (1996) *Researching into Teaching Methods in Colleges and Universities*, London: Kogan Page
Brown, G and Desforges, C (1979) *Piaget's Theory: A psychological critique*, London: Routledge and Kegan Paul.
Brown, J S, Collins, A and Duguid, P (1989) 'Situated cognition and the culture of learning', *Educational Researcher*, 18, 1, 32–42.
Bruner, J S (1966) *Towards a Theory of Instruction*, Cambridge, MA: Harvard University Press.
Bruner, J S (1985) 'Vygotsky: a historical and conceptual perspective' in Wertsch, J V (ed.) *Culture, Communication and Cognition: Vygotskyian perspectives*, Cambridge: Cambridge University Press.
Bruner, J S (1986) *Actual Minds, Possible Worlds*, Cambridge, MA: Harvard University Press.
Clarke, J A (1993) 'Cognitive style and computer assisted learning: problems and a possible solution', *Association for Learning Technology*, 1, 1, 47–59.
Entwistle, N J (1981) *Styles of Learning and Teaching: An integrated outline of educational psychology for students, teachers and lecturers*, New York: John Wiley.
Flavell, J H (1963) *The Developmental Psychology of Jean Piaget*, London: Van Nostrand.
Ford, N (1985) 'Learning styles and strategies of postgraduate students', *British Journal of Educational Technology*, 16, 1, 17–26 .
Gagné, R M (1975) *Essentials of Learning for Instruction*, Hillsdale, NJ: Dryden.
Gagné, R M (1977) *The Conditions of Learning*, New York: Holt, Rhinehart and Winston.
Gagné, R M (1982) 'Developments in learning psychology: implications for instructional design; and effects of computer technology on instructional design and development', *Educational Technology*, June, 11–15.
Gagné, R M and Briggs, L J (1979) *Principles of Instructional Design*, New York: Holt, Rhinehart and Winston.

Glaser, R (ed.) (1987) *Advances in Instructional Psychology Volume 3*, Hillsdale, NJ: Lawrence Erlbaum Associates.

Glass, G V (1976) 'Primary, secondary and meta-analysis research', *Educational Research*, 5, 3–8.

Glass, G V, McGaw, B and Smith, M L (1981) *Meta-analysis in Social Research*, Beverley Hills, CA: Sage.

Harel, I and Papert, S (1992) 'Software design as a learning environment', in Balestri, D, Ehrmann, S C and Ferguson, D (eds) *Learning to Design, Designing to Learn: Using technology to transform the curriculum*, London: Taylor and Francis.

Hodgson, V E, Mann, S J and Snell, R S (eds) (1987) *Beyond Distance Teaching – Towards Open Learning*, Buckingham: Open University Press.

Johnson, D C and Samways, B (eds) (1993) *Informatics and Changes in Learning*, Amsterdam: North Holland.

Jonassen, D (ed.) (1988) *Instructional Designs for Microcomputer Courseware*, Hillsdale, NJ: Lawrence Erlbaum Associates.

Jones, A and Mercer, N (1993) 'Theories of learning and information technology', in Scrimshaw, P (ed.) (1993) *Language, Classrooms and Computers*, London: Routledge.

Kogan, N (1971) 'Educational implications of cognitive styles' in Lesser, G S (ed.) *Psychology and Educational Practice*, Chicago, Ill.: Scott Foreman.

Kolb, D A (1984) *Experiential Learning*, NJ: Prentice-Hall.

Kulik, J A (1994) 'Meta-analytic studies of findings on computer-based instruction', in Baker, E L and O'Neil, H F, Jr (eds) *Technology Assessment in Education and Training*, Hillsdale, NJ: Lawrence Erlbaum Associates.

Kulik, J A and Kulik, C L C (1989) 'Meta-analysis in education', *International Journal of Educational Research*, 13, 221–340.

Laurillard, D (1993) *Rethinking University Teaching: A framework for the effective use of educational technology*, London: Routledge.

Lewis, R and Paine, N (1986) *How to Find and Adapt Materials and Select Media*, London: Council for Educational Technology.

MacDonald, B, Atkin, R, Jenkins, D and Kemmis, S (1977) 'Computer assisted learning: its educational potential', in Hooper, R (ed.) *The National Development Programme in Computer Assisted Learning: Final report of the director*, London: Council for Educational Technology.

Marton, F and Säljö, R (1976) 'On qualitative differences in learning II: outcome as a function of the learner's conception of the task', *British Journal of Educational Psychology*, 46, 115–27.

Mercer, N (1990) 'Researching common knowledge: studying the content and context of educational discourse', in Walford, G (ed.) *Doing Educational Research*, London: Routledge.

Merrill, D (1985) 'Where is the author in authoring?', *Journal of Computer Based Instruction*, 12, 4, 90–96.

Messick, S (1970) 'The criterion problem in the evaluation of instruction: assessing possible, not just intended outcomes', in Wittrock, M C and Wiley, D E (eds) *The Evaluation of Instruction: Issues and Problems*, New York: Holt Rhinehart and Winston.

Messick, S (1984) 'The nature of cognitive style: problems and promises in educational practice', *Educational Psychologist*, 19, 2, 59–74.

Newman, D, Griffin , P and Cole, M (1989) *The Construction Zone: Working for cognitive change in school,* Cambridge, Cambridge University Press.

National Organisation for Adult Learning (NOAL) (1993) *An Adult Higher Education: A vision,* Leicester: National Institute of Adult Continuing Education (NIACE).

Papert, S (1980) *Mindstorms: Children, computers and powerful ideas,* Brighton: Harvester.

Pask, G (1973) *Educational Methods using Information about Individual Styles and Strategies of Learning,* final report of the SSRC Project HR 1424/1, London: Social Science Research Council.

Pask, G (1976) 'Styles and strategies of learning', *British Journal of Educational Psychology,* 46, 128–48.

Pask, G and Scott, B C E (1972) 'Learning strategies and individual competence', *International Journal of Man-Machine Studies,* 4, 217–53.

Perkins, D N and Salomon, G (1989) 'Are cognitive skills context-bound?', *Educational Researcher,* 18, 16–25.

Piaget, J (1971) *Science of Education and the Psychology of the Child,* New York: Viking.

Ramsden, P (1992) *Learning to Teach in Higher Education,* London: Routledge.

Reigeluth, C M (1983) *Instructional Design Theories and Models: An overview of their current status,* Hillsdale, NJ: Lawrence Erlbaum Associates.

Sewell, D (1990) *New Tools for New Minds,* Brighton: Harvester Wheatsheaf.

Skinner, B F (1953) *Science and Human Behaviour,* London: Macmillan.

Smith, E (1990) *The Librarian, the Scholar and the Future of the Research Library,* Connecticut: Greenwood Press.

Tesch, R (1990) *Qualitative Research: Analysis types and software tools,* London: Falmer Press.

Vygotsky, L S (1978) *Mind in Society: The development of higher psychological processes,* Cambridge, MA: Harvard University Press.

Wengraf, T (1995) 'Towards empowering undergraduate students as action researchers into student learning', in Smith, B and Brown, S (eds) *Research Teaching and Learning in Higher Education,* London: Kogan Page.

Wertsch, J V (1985) *Vygotsky and the Social Formation of Mind,* Cambridge, MA: Harvard University Press.

Witkin, H A (1976) 'Cognitive style in academic performance and in teacher-student relations', in Messick, S *et al.* (eds) *Individuality in Learning,* San Francisco, CA: Jossey-Bass.

Witkin, H A, Moore, C A, Goodenough, D R and Cox, P W (1977) 'Field-dependent and field-independent cognitive styles and their educational implications', *Review of Educational Research,* 47, 1, 1–64.

Wolf, F M (1986) *Meta-analysis: Quantitative methods for research synthesis,* Beverley Hills, CA: Sage.

Chapter 5

Student Needs and Considerations

Introduction

The continuing pace of educational change and the need for diverse learning resources to meet changing demands necessitate variety and flexibility. The location of students' learning, the way they are taught, the style of approach and the sequence of development can vary. Students may learn by reading, visualizing, writing and doing. Learning resources need to allow for this diversity. In this chapter we look at differing student needs. We outline some of the issues involved in student access to information, including access for students with learning difficulties, physical disability and other special educational needs. We look at some materials available to support special needs and study skills. An issue growing in importance is the delivery of resources and support to students studying at a distance or part-time. We explore the student experience of resource-based learning and the growth of student power in the market place.

Background

Students require adequate access to learning resources. Follett (1993) reports a 1992 Quality in Higher Education Project national survey that used a questionnaire to students and staff to assess the most important factors contributing to quality, across all subject areas and types of institution. Of a total of 111 criteria identified, three of the top five related to library and allied services. The study highlighted the importance of access to library facilities (in terms of time and location); resourcing of libraries to cater for the needs of students and teaching staff; and staffing and IT facilities.

More students in secondary schools, particularly in classes working for external examinations, are becoming familiar with various forms of resource-based learning (RBL) and active learning. This means colleges and higher education institutions need to be aware of and exploit these skills within their existing and evolving course structures. With, for instance, increased modularization, credit accumulation and transfer schemes, and the accreditation of prior learning, the significance of which learning resources to use and when becomes more important.

Students are individuals with diverse learning experiences. They will develop their own preferred learning styles. One student may routinely work in the library, another prefers to work at home. Some students find continual assessment helpful, others perform better with final exams. The use of resources themselves is likely to reveal many variations. Gardner (1993) suggests that there are a variety of intelligences: linguistic, mathematical, visual, musical, physical, inter-personal and intrapersonal. You might suggest others such as auditory, manual or emotional. Students learn most effectively when they are given the resource that best corresponds to their natural learning medium. Some students learn quickest from a video, others from a text which consists mostly of diagrams or mathematical equations.

The ability to study effectively is a skill and that skill once gained is, in effect, a learning resource. The ability to manage time, processes and content with confidence, allows an individual to be flexible and self-assured in their learning. Effective use of resources and open-based learning require this skill.

RESEARCH TASK. INVESTIGATING THE RELATIONSHIPS BETWEEN COURSE STRUCTURE, STUDENT STUDY SKILLS AND THE USE OF RESOURCES

The purpose of this task is to investigate in some detail the relationships between course structure, student study skills and the use of resources, by tracking a student through a common learning task.

Take one element of your course and compile the following information about it:

- aims and objectives of this element as conveyed to the students and any information they may receive about assessment priorities;
- synopsis of the information relevant to this element delivered through direct instruction in lectures or seminars;
- the range of other resources to which students are directed, either through reading lists or through freer investigation in the library or resource centre. You can establish the latter through analysis of student essay bibliographies or through investigation yourself in the library or resource centre, possibly with a member of the library staff;

- the product which you require the student to create in order to prove they have understood the course, eg, essay, project, presentation.

Establish the skills required to produce the coursework product. Discover this through doing the assignment yourself and through asking students to keep a research diary of activities such as finding information, using it for specific tasks and evaluating its usefulness. Study the diaries to assess the effectiveness or otherwise of the students' use of resources.

Analyse:

- the kinds of information students seek from non-academic staff;
- what areas of your support could be constructively delegated to them;
- whether there are areas of student support which could be more effectively managed by support staff.

In many institutions, students are becoming cast in the role of customers and consumers. Some may be self-funding with a financial stake in the services they are receiving. You may wish to investigate the perceptions tutors have about the students as consumers and their awareness of a change in their relationship with the students. You could explore whether staff resent students becoming consumers or whether they accept that students have a right to complain.

RBL offers flexibility to a student but it needs to operate effectively in practice. It requires staff who know what resources are available, how to access them and how to guide or navigate a student through the maze. Information technology in its widest sense, and databases in particular, play a significant role here. Networking information can be invaluable. Overall differentiation of student needs can be built in to resource provision. Constructive learning is likely to be 'active, cumulative, goal-orientated, diagnostic and reflective' (Duffy *et al.*, 1993, p.291). Creating the learning environment is not in itself sufficient.

Students' learning resources needs may be defined by the demands of the course as it is constructed by academic staff, and depend on its design. Below we look at the resource implications of a few common patterns. These patterns may change at different stages of the course. It is common for fairly closely prescribed resource needs to widen, for example, if students do a self-selected extended essay or dissertation at the end of a taught course.

Patterns of Course Design
and their Resource Implications

1. The course is delivered by regular lectures or seminars in which all students on the course are taught the same thing at the same time. They are all given the same reading list and expected to follow prescribed readings throughout the course. Resource implications include:

- pressure on short-term access to resources with large numbers of students requiring the same material at the same time;
- resource needs are very clearly defined;
- resources collection development could focus on multiple copies of the set texts rather than a broad range of material;
- restrictions are usually imposed on library access to the resources, generally by providing a shorter loan period and imposing fines for late return.

2. Students are given much more freedom in their choice of assignments. They might for example be allowed to choose from a range of given essay titles or projects within a broad area. They might be allowed to choose their own topic. A number of broad areas might be taught concurrently which would further widen the range of topics they could choose. Resource implications include:

- less pressure on specific resources, as need becomes more individualized;
- resource needs are much more difficult to predict;
- resources collection development could focus on a broader range of material with fewer copies of each;
- the library could choose to adopt an 'access not holdings' strategy whereby material required rarely and on an individual basis is borrowed from other service suppliers;
- information skills would become much more important for the students to enable them to track down and evaluate for themselves the information resources they need.

3. On some courses the teacher may have decided to use a very narrow range of resources. Perhaps there is a key text which provides all the information necessary for a vocational or technical course. Resource implications include:

- extremely high pressure on access to that text, unless students are required and able to purchase it or have access to the loan of class sets for the period of the course;

- the need to provide any form of resource collection might be avoided altogether;
- students may remain unfamiliar with using a library collection.

Shortfalls in Resources Provision

Gibbs *et al.* (1994) describe the increasing problems in meeting student needs experienced by higher and further education in the UK with higher student numbers and class sizes, reduced per capita funding and resulting threats to quality, shortfalls in library provision and increased student diversity:

> The recent Follett report has highlighted the situation libraries have found themselves in as demand has increased, the cost of books and journals has risen (doubled and tripled, respectively, in real terms in a decade) and student purchases of their own books has declined. Library space per student has declined at the same time that changing teaching methods have placed more emphasis on independent study. Traditional libraries are now incapable of supporting traditional patterns of study involving 'reading for a degree'. In many large courses students' most common experience is that the items on their reading list are simply not available. If students are to do anything productive with the increasing proportion of 'out of class' learning time then new ways must be found to provide them with the necessary learning resources and with somewhere to study them. (Gibbs *et al.*, 1994, pp.7–8)

The authors conclude by suggesting that in many contexts radical alternatives to traditional course delivery are necessary if quality is to be rescued. We would argue that in many institutions there may still be some room for improving the effectiveness of resource provision through a reflective analysis of the patterns of resource needs and targeting of provision. To take a simple and common example: most teaching staff prepare some kind of reading list for their students and send it to the library for purchase consideration. Problems arise if the list is sent to the library late. It is easy to underestimate the time needed to order and process material. Even in a well staffed, well funded and efficient library it could take several weeks for material to be acquired even if that material is put into a fast stream through the process. Distributors often charge a premium for urgent action orders. Unfortunately reading lists may arrive in the library at the same time as the students requiring the material. We would suggest that available financial resources can be optimized by a careful evaluation and communication of the resource needs defined by a course. Once those needs are clearly articulated, strategies can be devised for meeting them and cost-implications can be more clearly understood. Effective communication with resource providers and those responsible for funding arrangements is essential.

The Follett report suggests that:

> Effective cooperation between teaching staff and the library is vital if both students and their teachers are to obtain the full benefit of the library service. In order to achieve this, teachers must play a part in ensuring that their own needs and those of their students are properly communicated to and understood by library staff. This point was made in the Parry Report in 1967 but is still insufficiently applied. (Follett, 1993, p.37)

Many institutions and individual teachers have sought new ways to ensure that students have adequate access to learning resources. You might like to consider to what extent the following approaches might be helpful to your students. You might use the techniques of cost-effectiveness analysis to compare them (This approach is discussed later in this chapter.)

Readers

A reader is a collection of copyright-cleared documents put together in a duplicated pack to provide the core reading for the course. It may contain chapters from books and journal articles. It may contain only reading material or it may have linking sections written by the lecturer, questions to guide reading and an extended bibliography. Students can be lent the reader for the duration of the course or they can buy it. The main barrier to the production of course readers is the need to obtain and pay for copyright permission. Costs can be high and organizing copyright clearance can be complicated and time-consuming. An evaluation of the potential of this approach would need to compare the costs of providing the same information in a traditional way.

Exley and Gibbs (1994) suggest that developments in electronic publishing have made it easier to put together customized readers from existing material for small print runs. Some publishers are now exploiting this and encourage academics to select and collate extracts from existing books to create readers at modest cost.

Using readers does not necessarily affect the extent to which students read widely. This would depend on how they were presented to the students and whether the use of other resources was reflected in assessments of students work. In considering the appropriateness of this form of resourcing for your courses, you might like to look at the way readers are used at the School of Education, Oxford Brookes University (Parsons and Gibbs,1994, p.34ff). An alternative to readers are reading sets where a single copy of the collected material is kept together, perhaps in a box-file, for loan or reference to students. Exley and Gibbs suggest that such collections could focus on particular course topics and assignments could be rotated so that the resources are under less pressure.

Course Material Produced within the Institution

Many institutions have worked to produce resources themselves (for examples see Gibbs *et al.*, 1994). You might like to investigate the potential for producing material within your institution.

Advantages of this approach include:

- course material can be closely matched to your course needs;
- copyright is owned by you or the institution so material can be copied and adapted at very low cost;
- you might be able to sell or share the materials with other institutions;
- interesting materials can be produced relatively cheaply within an institution if you have enough time and access to computers and printers. Audio-visual and sophisticated reprographic facilities and technical staff with expertise would all be very helpful.

Disadvantages include:

- such production can be very time-consuming – not every institution will recognize and pay for such work, thus taking time away from other activities such as direct teaching or research which might be better rewarded;
- students may be put off by poorly produced materials;
- the possible lack of breadth of information provided;
- it may be much more cost-effective to adapt existing materials.

Writing resource materials, even on a very small scale, can be a very interesting project. Writing material yourself may help you develop a clear idea of what makes a good or a bad learning resource and how to adapt existing materials to support your students. Race (1992) provides some useful suggestions and guidelines for producing learning resources.

Access to Resources for Distance and Part-time Students

Traditional resource services to students sometimes assume that students will be able to spend considerable periods of time at a central resource supply. Many institutions have found that as part-time courses increase and distance learning becomes more common, adaptations need to be made so that distance and part-time students are not disadvantaged.

Students may find it hard to get to a central resource supply. This might be because of geographical distance or because students who are also working full- or part-time will be unable to visit the library when it is open. Opening hours may be restricted at weekends or evenings. Timetabling arrangements for part-time students may not allow sufficient time for students to visit the library when they attend college and they may find it difficult to make special journeys.

Many libraries have introduced restrictions on the loan of material as a means of ensuring that access to scarce resources is shared among students. Arrangements such as reference and short loan collections are likely to cause problems for students who have limited time to spend in the library and who, because they are not visiting the campus every day, would have difficulty in returning short loan or overnight material when due.

Students who use a library or resource centre regularly will become familiar with the organization of services and materials and could put into practice any induction training provided. Students who do not have this advantage may find that they are not able to get the most from available resources. It is important not to underestimate the potential of libraries to bewilder their users. Pressures of time on part-time and distance courses make it necessary to ensure that adequate time is allocated to study and information skills. Distance and part-time learners may need this support even more than other students.

In identifying and addressing the resources needs of students, including distance and part-time students, a useful approach is the self-advocacy model (see Ashcroft *et al.*, 1996 for more details). Students can be asked to identify any difficulties they might be experiencing and to make their own suggestions for ways these could be addressed.

RESEARCH TASK. USING SELF-ADVOCACY TO IMPROVE RESOURCE PROVISION FOR DISTANCE AND PART-TIME STUDENTS

There are various ways in which student views can be sought. You might like to consider the following approach.

Following discussion with your students, have them determine the appropriate issues to be investigated and have them devise the questions to be raised in a questionnaire. You might recommend to them that it is useful to be clear and unambiguous in what you are asking and to make the questionnaire as short and user-friendly as possible in order to maximize responses. Questions could be given in a mixture of open and closed format.

Closed questions prescribe the response required. The advantage of this kind of question is that it is easier to analyse responses. For instance the students might ask questions to do with the library and its opening hours, such as:

- Is the library open at times when it is convenient for you to visit it? Please circle the response which most closely matches your opinion.
  Never   Rarely   Sometimes   Usually   Frequently
- Please grade the usefulness of the following options for extended opening hours with the least useful being graded 5 and the most useful 1:
  ..... Very late opening, once a month, until 11pm
  ..... Longer opening hours once a week, the day you attend your course
  ..... Longer opening hours every evening in the week
  ..... Longer opening hours at the weekend
  ..... Longer opening hours in the college vacation.

Open questions allow respondents more freedom to express their opinions. Answers can be much more informative, but, especially from large groups, can be difficult to analyse. Examples of open questions include:

- What problems have you found in obtaining material for your most recent assignment?
- What would make your access to learning resources easier?

The students could then help to interpret the results in pairs, groups or collectively and suggest possible courses of action.

You could then compare the process and outcomes of this approach with that of a more traditional survey generated by the tutor.

Institutions have adopted a range of measures to address distance and part-time student needs. The Open University, for example, has constructed study packs which contain all the material that is required reading for that course. Some libraries are now setting up specific long-term loan collections for distance learners and named contacts who will assist in locating and delivering materials. Learners may be encouraged to form local groups who can share a mini-library loaned and refreshed occasionally by the central resource supply. Collaborative arrangements with libraries local to the student may help in the support of distance learners.

Computers and Distance Learners

Nipper (1989) describes a development of three generations of distance learning linked to types of resources, drawing from experience of distance education in Denmark. He suggests that correspondence teaching is a first generation, using written or printed material as the medium. Since the late 1960s a second generation has emerged with the increasing use of print plus broadcast media, cassettes and a gradually increasing use of computers. The model of learning used in both generations is a behaviourist one. The third generation is based on new technologies that increase interactivity between tutors and learners and provide a channel of communication between learners. It is suggested that the implementation of computer conferencing can move the locus of control in distance education from the teacher and the teaching material to the group and the processes generated from the group, with a less authoritarian role for the institution and the tutor. Many distance learners are professionals having considerable experience and expertise to share with other course members. Computer conferencing can facilitate the sharing of this valuable resource and can provide peer contact which may be lacking in conventional distance courses.

Evaluating Distance Learning

One possible area for research is the evaluation of a distance learning programme. Reflective tutors will carry out informal evaluation during face-to-face sessions with students and will use a multitude of sources of information to aid decisions to amend the teaching during the session, and later to improve the teaching and learning by modifying the approach or materials to be used. In a distance learning programme this is not possible in the same way and so there is a need for formal evaluation, using a variety of techniques, to determine the effectiveness of the programme and also to inform development to enhance the delivery of the instruction and the quality of learning. Also, as distance learning is increasingly involved with various forms of technology, an evaluation can be made of how the use of these technologies may increase access.

Evaluation of this type can take two forms. *Formative* evaluation is about making judgements during a programme with the purpose of identifying possible changes that can be made to improve the programme and make it more likely to achieve its intended aims. Typical questions that might be asked would be, What has happened so far? How are we doing? What should we do next? Should we change anything? *Summative* evaluation on the other hand is concerned with describing the results of a programme, and assessing its effectiveness after it has finished. Typical questions here would be, Did the programme achieve its aims? Were the aims appropriate? What did not work? Is it worth doing again?

Clarke (1994) provides a very good overview of the evaluation of distance learning programmes based on a report commissioned by the US Office of Technology Assessment in 1988. In it he argues that evaluation of distance learning programmes should differentiate between 'delivery' technology and 'instructional' technology. Delivery technologies are to do with the equipment and media involved, and the educational technologies involved come from research in the physical sciences. Chacon (1992) describes various technologies used in distance education. Instructional technologies on the other hand are products of social science and psychological research into teaching and learning, and are the instructional design theories and teaching methods that can be used when creating instructional materials.

Many evaluations have failed to distinguish between the two, and incorrectly attributed benefits to one type of technology which were actually due to the other, with expensive consequences. There is much debate about whether specific educational media have an influence *per se* on learning outcomes. Clarke (1983; 1994) maintains that the weight of research shows that media are purely vehicles for delivery and do not influence learning, but others (see for example Kozma, 1991) argue that the case is not proven and that as learners actively collaborate with a given medium to construct their knowledge, there may be intrinsic benefits to using particular media.

You might consider gathering participant reaction. This can be used for both formative and summative purposes. Interviews are the richest source of qualitative data and one way of interviewing distance learners is to use a telephone survey. You might use a structured interview with a protocol consisting of a sequence of linked questions, with the answer to one question determining which question is asked next (see for example Thorpe, 1988). Such interviews take time and questionnaires can also be used to gather very rich data, if a mixture of open and closed questions are used.

RESEARCH TASK. QUESTIONNAIRE SURVEY

Develop a questionnaire to discover the reactions of participants on your distance learning programme.
Design questions that focus on each of:

- the materials used;
- the assignments set;
- the tuition given;
- the methods used (eg, workshops, group meetings, e-mail, conferencing).

In your analysis of the responses discriminate between items dealing with the delivery media and items dealing with the instructional techniques employed.
Use a number of different question strategies:

- first a closed question to focus attention on a topic and prompt the respondent ('Please rate the teaching of this part of the course as exceptional, average or poor') then a follow up allowing them an open-ended response to expand on their answer ('Please give some examples of how particular topics were taught, to explain your response');
- open-ended questions concentrating on particular elements of the course;
- questions asking for non-specific open-ended overview comments ('List what you think are the strong and weak points of the programme').

The learner feedback gathered may lead to ideas for a study guide or advance organizer (see Chapter 6) to help future users of the materials.
There are many books which deal with the design of questionnaires and the analysis of the responses obtained. Oppenheim (1992) is a classic on questionnaire design. Mitton (1982) is an excellent guide to methods of processing data. Bennett et al. (1996) discuss uses of IT to process data. Another point to bear in mind is the sample of participants to survey; see Cohen and Mannion (1994) or Fowler (1984) for a discussion of sample sizes and sampling theory.

Another area for evaluation is the level of achievement of the programme's objectives. Here again you can discriminate between delivery and instructional objectives. Typical delivery technology objectives would be assessments of the reliability of the equipment and evaluations of the extent to which the media were successful in opening up student access to new courses. Instructional technology objectives could include changes in student knowledge, increases in motivation, and the ability to transfer skills and knowledge to other contexts. These could be evaluated by an assessment of assignments set for the students in terms of submission rates and performance. However, care must be taken in drawing conclusions from evidence based on comparisons with students following similar courses but in different modes. You will need to ask questions about the comparability of the two groups.

Another area for investigation might be to find out which instructional methods had most effect. You could use some of the ideas discussed in Chapter 4. You might look at whether participants prefer structured and guided materials to more open-ended discovery learning approaches. You might also investigate which materials addressed which types of knowledge in terms of the taxonomy developed in Chapter 6, and in particular whether higher order thinking skills developed. This is a difficult question to investigate but some tests to measure problem-solving and study skill development have been developed (see Congress of the US, 1988; and Levin and Meister, 1985).

A final area of investigation, but a very important one, is that of the cost-effectiveness of a distance learning programme. Cost-effectiveness analysis combines a calculation of costs with an assessment of achievement of intended outcomes to produce a measure that allows comparison of possible alternative approaches to particular learning requirements. There are many methods of carrying out such analysis but the Ingredients Method outlined in Levin (1983; 1988) is particularly suited to the kinds of programmes we are considering. It involves identification of all the ingredients required for the programme, a costing of these ingredients and a summation of these costs. This cost is then allied to measures of effectiveness such as programme completion rates, test scores from assessments, measures of student satisfaction and so on.

Gaining a more complete picture of the cost-effectiveness of a programme requires attempting to quantify all the costs implicit in it, not just the obvious ones, and the measurements of effectiveness which are particularly suited to an educational context. Some interesting results may be obtained. For example, when considering delivery technology, a solution employing traditional technologies such as teachers, books and the postal system may be cheaper than a computer solution to a problem. Evaluation studies have shown (Levin, 1983) that teachers can be much cheaper than computers for certain instructional tasks, even simple drill-and-practice exercises where the computer solution might have been thought preferable.

When considering instructional technologies, you need to consider time costs as well as monetary costs:

> In some applications, the cheapest and/or quickest options are not necessarily the best. Students who learn cheaper or faster do not necessarily learn better. The new 'cognitive' learning theories provide the insight that it may be more important to know how students reach learning goals than to know that they get correct answers in examinations. It often takes longer for students to learn in such a way that their correct answer on a test reflects 'deep cognitive processing' and the exercise of higher order cognitive learning skills, than to take a surface level shortcut. Educators need to be wary of focusing evaluations on time savings at the expense of the quality of learning. (Clarke, 1994, p.75)

For further discussion of these ideas of 'deep' and 'surface' approaches to learning, see Chapter 6.

We have indicated many elements that need to be taken into account when providing a distance learning programme. Rowntree (1992) gives a comprehensive discussion of the theory and practice of open and distance learning. It is itself designed as an open learning text, and contains useful checklists to guide a prospective programme provider through each stage of course design and delivery, including the costing process.

Students with Specific Learning Needs

The library and other learning resources can be very difficult to use for students with a wide range of disabilities, including dyslexia, blindness, deafness, mobility-impairment and so on. There are many things which can be done to make life easier such as special magnification readers and books-on-tape for the sight-impaired, or ramps and lifts for wheelchair users. Resource centres may not address the issues because until you are serving students with difficulties there seems little point in investing for them. On the other hand students will be deterred from applying to institutions without such assistance programmes and facilities.

STUDENT NEEDS AND CONSIDERATIONS

You may need to discover which disabilities your resource centre can cater for, whether it is routinely informed if disabled students are recruited and whether management are aware of the specific problems and potential remedies for disabled students in order to assess whether disabled people are encouraged or discouraged from applying.

Students' learning difficulties may be relatively mild; for example a student may experience difficulty with the written coursework or the mathematical component of the course. Specific difficulties like these may be addressed by a remedial centre or by 'surgeries' using the teaching staff on particular courses.

You might decide to survey your students and discover if they have experienced difficulties with certain tasks. You could look at how they addressed the problems; for instance through peer assistance, through your department, through yourself or through a centrally run service.

RESEARCH TASK. INVESTIGATING
DISABLED STUDENTS' NEEDS

If you have students with specific disabilities there may be special interest groups which you can contact for assistance. For example in the UK there are the National Bureau for Students with Disabilities, Research Centre for the Education of the Visually Handicapped, and the Royal National Institute for Deaf People. (See Ashcroft et al., 1996, for a fuller list of agencies that may be able to supply information or help to students with special needs.)

Good general directories can provide you with this information. The UK Association of Teachers and Lecturers (1994) has produced a useful handbook which includes a number of information sources. Conduct a literature search to discover relevant background information. Contact national funding bodies; they will be able to advise on guidelines for provision and may be able to identify sources of grant money for the development of facilities.

Investigate the needs of one of your students with a form of disability affecting their learning. For instance, talk to students with sight problems and together consider:

- criteria for directing the student to relevant resources;
- how you can make use of video-work and the OHP;
- how to develop your use of worksheet approaches;
- the forms of equipment available to help, or how working with another student could be explored;
- ways of accessing information from the Internet;
- the use of CD-ROM sound facilities.

It is important that any research concerning students with specific disabilities is not 'done' to the subjects. They will know more about their needs than

---

107

you will. There is a wealth of literature criticizing researchers who disempower already relatively powerless groups by doing research *on* them, rather than *with* them.

You could discuss with the students their view of the role of resources in their learning and publish your findings for a journal as a piece of insider action research.

There are students whose learning needs may not be obvious. For instance, those who have not studied for a considerable length of time may have lost, or never even acquired, the necessary specialist vocabulary associated with their area of study. Such students can suffer from what has been called 'information anxiety' (Wurman, 1990). A mixture of embarrassment, confusion, ignorance, carelessness and over-confidence can lead to misapplication of time and effort when it comes to them using the resources available. Approaches to dealing with this are as crucial as the resources themselves.

RESEARCH TASK. TACKLING SPECIFIC STUDENT NEEDS

Draw up a checklist of factors which are particularly pertinent to a range of students who have various learning needs, and require specific attention if there is to be an effective role for them on your course in a resource context. Together with these students identify this list, for example:

- location and availability of resources;
- time to access the resources;
- presentation format of resources;
- confidence to use the resources.

Together, assess the changes needed to meet the requirements of certain students. For example:

- see how far a group of physically handicapped students can take advantage of resources in a designated room;
- give what you perceive to be appropriate time for those students with limited IT skills to complete an IT-based assignment and together judge whether the time allocation was appropriate;
- devise an expected presentation style for students with hearing impairment which revolves around use of visual displays and together assess its appropriateness;
- create a groupwork exercise involving mature students such as collecting and collating information from a range of on-line resources and giving a presentation on their findings and together consider whether such methods actually met their needs.

After completion of the tasks discuss with the students the factors you took into account and see if their experiences matched your attempt to meet their perceived needs. Consider disseminating the responses and your analysis to colleagues and the appropriate managers within your institution.

Summary

Students' needs and considerations are as diverse as the potential learning resources available to meet them. Researching the two together can reveal the pattern of availability and the gaps to be filled. It also involves assessing the whole resource environment from a number of angles, which is an issue of some significance as will be seen in the next chapter.

Annotated Reading List

Smith, E (1990) *The Librarian, the Scholar and the Future of the Research Library*, Connecticut: Greenwood Press.
Very good in looking at the role of the research librarian in relation to the information needs of students.
Meyer, C and Jones, TB (1993) *Promoting Active Learning: Strategies for the college classroom*, San Francisco, CA: Jossey-Bass.
Useful in looking at the skills involved in active learning and in stimulating ideas for research into these skills through use of resources.

References

Ashcroft, K, Bigger, S and Coates, D (1996) *Researching into Equal Opportunities in Colleges and Universities*, London: Kogan Page.
Association of Teachers and Lecturers (ATL) (1994) *Achievement for All*, London: ATL.
Bennett, C, Foreman-Peck, L and Higgins, C (1996) *Researching into Teaching Methods in Colleges and Universities*, London: Kogan Page.
Chacon, F (1992) 'A taxonomy of computer media in distance education', *Journal of Open and Distance Learning*, 7, 1, 12–27.
Clarke, R E (1983) 'Reconsidering research on learning from media', *Review of Educational Research*, 53, 4, 445–59.
Clarke, R E (1994) 'Assessment of distance learning technology', in Baker, E L and O'Neil, H F, Jr (eds) *Technology Assessment in Education and Training*, Hillsdale, NJ: Lawrence Erlbaum Associates.

Cohen, L and Mannion, L (1994) *Research Methods in Education,* London: Routledge.

Congress of the US, Office of Technology Assessment (1988) Power On: New tools for teaching and learning, Washington, DC: US Government Printing Office.

Duffy, T M, Lowyck, J and Jonassen, D H (eds) (1993) *Designing Environments for Constructive Learning,* Berlin: Springer-Verlag.

Exley, K and Gibbs, G (1994) *Course Design for Resource-based Learning: Science,* Oxford: The Oxford Centre for Staff Development, Oxford Brookes University.

Follett, B (Chairman) (1993) *Joint Funding Council's Libraries Review Group: Report,* Bristol: Higher Education Funding Council for England.

Fowler, F (1984) *Survey Research Methods,* Beverley Hills, CA: Sage.

Gardner, H (1993) *Frames of Mind: The theory of multiple intelligences,* London: Fontana.

Gibbs, G, Pollard, N and Farrell, J (1994) *Institutional Support for Resource-based Learning,* Oxford: The Oxford Centre for Staff Development, Oxford Brookes University.

Kozma, R (1991) 'Learning with media', *Review of Educational Research,* 61, 2, 179–211.

Levin, H (1983) *Cost-effectiveness: A primer,* Beverley Hills, CA: Sage.

Levin, H (1988) 'The economics of computer-assisted instruction', *Peabody Journal of Education,* May.

Levin, H and Meister, G (1985) *Educational Technology and Computers: Promises, promises always promises,* Stanford, CA: Center for Educational Research, Stanford University.

Mitton, R (1982) *Practical Research in Distance Teaching: A handbook for developing countries,* Cambridge: International Extension College.

Nipper, S (1989) 'Third generation distance learning and computer conferencing', in Mason, R and Kaye, A (eds) *Mindweave: Communication, computers and distance education,* Oxford: Pergamon.

Oppenheim, A N (1992) *Questionnaire Design, Interviewing and Attitude Measurement,* London: Pinter.

Parsons, C and Gibbs, G (1994) *Course Design for Resource-based Learning: Education,* Oxford : The Oxford Centre for Staff Development, Oxford Brookes University.

Race, P (1992) *53 Interesting Ways to Write Open Learning Materials,* Bristol: Technical and Educational Services.

Rowntree, D (1992) *Exploring Open and Distance Learning,* London: Kogan Page.

Thorpe, M (1988) *Evaluating Open and Distance Learning,* Harlow: Longman.

Wurman, R S (1990) 'Information anxiety', in Lynch, M J and Young, A (eds) *Academic Libraries: Research perspectives,* Chicago, Ill.: American Library Association Publishers.

Chapter 6

Assessment of the Resource Environment

Where is the wisdom we have lost in knowledge?
Where is the knowledge we have lost in information?
(TS Eliot, *The Rock*)

Introduction

We have been developing the argument that the learning process in colleges and universities should consist of more than the transmission of information to students. Academic learning is about how a subject is known as well as what is known. It requires experience but also reflection on experience, carried out alone and in discussion with others. In concert with TS Eliot, we wish to draw a distinction between information, knowledge and wisdom. The *Oxford English Dictionary* defines information as 'something told, an item of knowledge', whereas knowledge is 'familiarity gained by experience, theoretical or practical understanding'. The implication to be drawn is that providing a student with the resources to amass information is not sufficient; there is a need for a development of understanding before the student can be said to have gained knowledge. For example, access to innumerable databases on the Internet from which to print out quantities of information will not of itself lead to a gain in understanding and knowledge of a topic. As Laurillard says, 'knowledge is information transformed – selected, analysed, interpreted, integrated, articulated, tested in application, evaluated' (Laurillard, 1993, p.123).

Further, wisdom may be defined as 'possession of experience and knowledge together with the power of applying them critically or practically'. So working through learning materials which develop an understanding of a topic, though beneficial, still leaves a need for opportunities to apply the knowledge, reflect on the outcomes and engage in critical discussion with others.

We argue that the provision of resources, be they traditional or modern computer-based materials, is just part of the story. They must be embedded in a rich teaching and learning environment. Having discussed the use and evaluation of particular learning resources, we now consider the learning environment as a whole. This consideration will encompass both the teaching and learning elements of the environment and its organization and management.

Approaches to Learning

A fundamental concept that has been identified by research into teaching and learning in higher education during the last 20 years, is the idea of a student's approach to learning. This will be of use to us when discussing and evaluating the learning environment we are hoping to create, so we will briefly review the salient points of the research (for a more detailed overview see, for example, Ramsden, 1992).

Various studies were carried out at Gothenburg University in Sweden into how students read academic texts. These were reported in a sequence of papers by Marton and Säljö (1976a; 1976b), Fransson (1977) and Svensson (1977). There is a very readable account of the work by two of the main researchers in Marton and Säljö (1984), including a useful discussion of the methods used in carrying out such a qualitative analysis. In general, the experiments showed that four different qualitative outcomes were observed in the students' levels of understanding of the texts, which could be identified by their types of response to questioning about the texts. These were:

Level A: Conclusion-orientated, detailed
  The student summarises the author's main argument, shows how evidence is used to support the argument, and explains the thoughts and reflections used to reach personal understanding of that argument.
Level B: Conclusion-orientated, mentioning
  Again there is an adequate summary of the main argument but the use of evidence or personal experience to support that argument is not made clear.
Level C: Description, detailed
  The student gives an adequate list of the main points presented in the article, but fails to show how these are developed into an argument.

Level D: Description, mentioning
A few isolated points are made, some relevant, others irrelevant. At the bottom end of this category an impression of confusion and misunderstanding is given by the student's comments. (Entwistle, 1981, based on Fransson, 1977 and Säljö, 1975)

The researchers explore how the different ways of understanding the text had come about. The students were interviewed, asked questions about the content of the texts, and also asked questions designed to discover how they had attempted the task. After intensive analysis of the verbatim transcripts of the interviews, the researchers found that those students who had failed to understand the argument in the text did so because they were not looking for a reasoned argument. The students essentially divided into two groups. For one group the process of learning focused on the text itself, whereas for the other the focus was on what the text was about. Of course some students could not be precisely placed into one group or the other (either because they showed some elements of both approaches, or else there was not enough information in their interview to decide either way) but in general terms the distinction could be made.

The first group did not try to understand the text; they effectively tried to memorize it. As Marton and Säljö put it in a memorable phrase: 'their awareness skated along the surface of the text'. However, for the second group, the text was seen as a means to an end. Their aim was to determine the author's intention underlying the text. These two approaches have come to be known respectively as the 'surface approach' and the 'deep approach' to learning.

The researchers found a striking relationship between the approach taken by the students and the level of understanding they displayed; see, for example, Table 6.1. The relationship is even more striking if we categorize levels A and B as high level understanding requiring some relation of evidence to conclusion, and levels C and D as low level understanding; this is shown in Table 6.2.

Table 6.1

Level of understanding	Approach to learning		
	Deep	Surface	Not clear
A	5	0	0
B	4	1	6
C	0	8	0
D	0	5	1

Table 6.2

Level of understanding	Approach to learning		
	Deep	Surface	Not clear
High	9	1	6
Low	0	13	1

Although this particular example is only a small sample, this close correlation of depth of approach to learning and quality of outcome has been confirmed many times (see, for example, van Rossum and Schenk, 1984). In his paper, Svensson (1977) argued that this conclusion is not surprising as a student may adopt a deep approach but not achieve a high level of understanding for any number of reasons, but it would be impossible for a student to adopt a surface approach and achieve a high level of understanding.

Deep Approach

These findings imply that we should ensure that the learning resources we provide encourage a deep approach to study. However, the question arises as to whether it is possible to influence a student's approach to learning. One possible idea would be to observe what characterizes the deep and surface approaches in a given learning situation, and then design learning resources that would influence students who do not normally adopt the deep approach to carry out the activities that characterized the deep approach. However, the indicators of the deep approach are symptoms of an attitude to learning, not an end in themselves. In one of the experiments, Marton and Säljö (1976b) investigated whether the outcomes required of students could influence their approach to the learning task. They showed that it was all too easy to influence students to adopt a surface approach; but when the intention was to influence the students to adopt a deep approach some of the group did, whereas others were led to a surface approach. They found that it depended on the individual student's interpretation of what was required of them.

Thus it would seem that one factor influencing the adoption of a particular approach to learning is that of individual motivation to learn. Fransson (1977) showed that the main effect on approach to learning in his study came from the reported experiences of the students – whether they felt interested, threatened or anxious. He concluded that interest (intrinsic motivation), absence of threat (extrinsic motivation) and absence of anxiety were associated with a deep approach, while threat, anxiety and absence of interest were associated with a surface approach.

However, the research now seemed to be developing a chicken and egg relationship between approach to learning and motivation to learn. Not having an interest in a text would tend to lead to a surface approach to learning, but a surface approach to learning would tend to prevent any interest in the text. Escape from this cycle requires the introduction of another frame of reference.

Säljö (1979) carried out interviews with students about what they understood by 'learning'. He was able to identify five qualitatively different conceptions of learning:

1. increasing knowledge;
2. memorizing information for reproduction;
3. acquiring facts, skills and procedures for later use;
4. making sense of or abstracting meaning from a situation;
5. interpreting and understanding reality.

A common feature of the first three is an element of reproduction of information and a feeling that learning is an external process, whereas the last two are qualitatively different and have a feeling of learning as an internal constructive process.

Van Rossum and Schenk (1984) undertook a study similar to the Gothenburg experiments to investigate, amongst other things, whether there was a relationship between a student's conception of learning and their approach to learning; their findings are shown in Table 6.3. Again, if we simplify the categories and (using van Rossum and Schenk's terminology) classify conceptions 1, 2, 3 as 'reproductive' and conceptions 4, 5 as 'constructive' the relationship is even more striking and reinforces the view that the student's conception of learning will also have an influence on their adoption of approach to learning; see Table 6.4.

Table 6.3

| Learning conception | Approach to learning | |
	Surface	Deep
1	6	0
2	19	4
3	8	7
4	1	11
5	1	12

Table 6.4

Learning conception	Approach to learning	
	Surface	*Deep*
reproductive	33	11
constructive	2	23

From this discussion we can see that the concepts of deep and surface learning approaches are very powerful and we can use them as a frame of reference for evaluating learning resources and their use. While the research shows that this categorization of approaches as either deep or surface is valid for most subjects, Ramsden (1992) discusses how what constitutes these approaches can vary according to academic discipline or task within that discipline. Many specific examples of the sorts of differences found in different disciplines are contained in Entwistle and Ramsden (1983). Before you can start to think in terms of these approaches you need to see what these general ideas mean in relation to your own subject.

RESEARCH TASK. DEEP AND SURFACE
APPROACHES TO LEARNING

Consider some tasks associated with your own discipline:

- essay writing;
- note taking, both in lectures and from texts;
- problem solving;
- report writing;
- practical work;
- exam revision.

Make a list of evidence that you consider would identify a deep or a surface approach for each of your tasks, for example, how factual detail is dealt with can exemplify an approach. Unrelated facts collected together for a single purpose to answer a particular problem or point may suggest a surface approach, whereas factual information placed in context, related to previous knowledge, and treated as part of a coherent whole would be evidence of a deep approach.

Ask colleagues both in your own discipline and in others to carry out the same process, and compare results with them. You might then discuss any differences between disciplines.

The Learning Environment

We now consider what constitutes the learning environment. In physical terms, it includes the resources we provide and the physical surroundings that they are to be used in. In social terms, it includes the teaching and learning methods that are to be used and the culture or ethos engendered for their use.

One way of starting to organize our ideas when researching and evaluating the learning environment is to follow Resnick (1983) and to distinguish three components which make up a theory of learning from instruction. In simple terms the three components which we can investigate are: what is to be learnt, how it is to be learnt and how it is to be taught. In more formal terms we can define them as:

- a theory of expertise which describes the knowledge and skills a student must acquire to become expert, that is to be able to perform competently in a given domain;
- a theory of acquisition which explains the processes of learning and development which are needed to achieve this expertise;
- a theory of intervention which describes the pedagogical processes, the teaching and learning methods to be used to encourage this learning and development.

The theory of expertise is perhaps the one that needs most comment as it is the area that has not been dealt with elsewhere. Here we are considering what we might term the content element of the environment. Much recent research in cognitive psychology has been concerned with the types of knowledge required for expertise. Many investigations into expert performance in a variety of domains have led to an emerging consensus of opinion about the concepts, facts and procedures component of expert performance and also the identification of various types of strategic knowledge which enable the expert to use the factual knowledge to perform tasks. This consensus has identified four categories of knowledge which can be summarized as follows (Collins *et al.*, 1991; de Corte, 1990):

Domain knowledge – this is a domain-specific knowledge base consisting of a well-organized collection of facts, concepts, rules, procedures and so on related to the particular subject in question.
Heuristic strategies – these are generally applicable techniques or expert rules of thumb for tackling tasks or problems. A classic example of these can be found in Polya (1945) which attempted to describe problem-solving heuristics in mathematics. These

included such approaches as: identifying known and unknown elements of a problem; looking for similar, related problems; looking for analogies; breaking a problem down into sub-problems; specializing; generalizing; using diagrams and special notations and so on – all elements of a mathematician's repertoire but discussed in a general context.

Control strategies – these are metacognitive skills, approaches to managing or controlling one's use of heuristic strategies and domain knowledge. They involve planning a solution strategy, monitoring the cognitive processes being carried out, deciding when to change tack and so on.

Learning strategies – these are activities and approaches that enable learners to develop any of the three preceding types of knowledge.

RESEARCH TASK. KNOWLEDGE TYPE AUDIT

Consider the courses in your area that a typical student would take. Carry out an audit of them in terms of inclusion of the four types of knowledge discussed.

Create a curriculum map of the courses with your findings shown diagrammatically to give a simple visual overview of the course content in terms of when, where and to what degree these elements are experienced by your students.

You might consider some of the following questions when you see the results.

- Are all four types of knowledge dealt with, and to what degree?
- When do they occur in the different courses?
- Do their occurrences mesh together well or do they clash?
- Is there an element of progression for the students' development when they do occur?

Ask a colleague to carry out the same task with the same material, and then analyse how useful the categories are as a means of analysing learning and whether they provide a vocabulary whose meaning can be fully shared in practice.

The ideas of a theory of acquisition have already been touched on in our discussion of theories of learning in Chapter 4. We looked at the processes of learning and development: the balance between discovery learning and personal exploration of a topic on the one hand and systematic instruction and guidance on the other; accommodation of different learning styles; the socio-cultural ideas of the influence of social interaction on learning and the zone of proximal development; the ideas of situated cognition and the power of anchoring learning in realistic contexts. We would also be concerned with the adoption of deep or surface approaches to learning as discussed at the beginning of this chapter. An interesting idea might be to consider the learning environment for one of your courses and to investigate whether the context the students are operating in is influencing them to adopt deep or surface approaches. Remember that the learning environment includes the resources we provide, the physical surroundings that they are to be used in, the teaching and learning methods that are to be used and the culture or ethos engendered for their use.

You could consider the learning environment for one of your courses and see if you can identify any characteristics of influences on deep or surface approaches to learning. Ramsden (1992, p.81) contains a useful summary of characteristics to look for. He suggests surface approaches are encouraged by:

- assessment methods emphasizing recall or the application of trivial procedural knowledge;
- assessment methods that create anxiety;
- cynical or conflicting messages about rewards;
- an excessive amount of material in the curriculum;
- poor or absent feedback on progress;
- lack of independence in studying;
- lack of interest in and background knowledge of the subject matter.

He suggests deep approaches are encouraged by:

- teaching and assessment methods that foster active and long-term engagement with learning tasks;
- stimulating and considerate teaching, especially teaching which demonstrates the lecturer's personal commitment to the subject matter and stresses its meaning and relevance to students;
- clearly stated academic expectations;
- opportunities to exercise responsible choice in the method and content of study;
- interest in and background knowledge of the subject matter.

As we have seen, it is very easy to influence students to adopt surface approaches to learning. You might consider how you could turn any of the negative influences in your course to positive influences for the deep approach.

The final element, the theory of intervention, is to do with the teaching and learning methods to be used. One approach to these comes from the realms of instructional psychology and is described in the 'cognitive apprenticeship' model as developed by Collins *et al.* (1989; 1991) which we shall discuss next. As they themselves admit, this is not a relevant model for all aspects of teaching, but you may find it useful for analysing your learning environment, bringing together as it does many of the elements we have been discussing.

A Framework for Designing Learning Environments

The basic ideas of cognitive apprenticeship are that learning is a constructive process and that the acquisition of knowledge and skills should take place in context. Collins *et al.* (1991) analysed a number of successful examples of teaching in the foundational domains of reading, writing and mathematics which had these elements in common – Palincsar and Brown's (1984) reciprocal teaching of reading, Scardamalia and Bereiter's (1985) procedural facilitation of writing, and Schoenfeld's (1985) teaching of mathematical problem solving. They then proposed the following abstract model of cognitive apprenticeship which encompassed all these, for use as a framework for designing powerful learning environments.

The model suggests four dimensions that make up a learning environment: the content taught, the pedagogical methods employed, the sequencing of learning activities, and the sociology of learning. The description of content they suggest has already been discussed in the previous section and consists of the four types of knowledge: domain knowledge, heuristic strategies, control strategies and learning strategies.

The teaching methods are based on an attempt to translate the features of traditional craft apprenticeship to the realms of academic learning. They identify six ways to promote the development of expert performance:

Modelling – the teacher performs a task so that the students can observe and build a conceptual model of the processes involved in carrying out a solution. In terms of the previous discussion on content, the teacher should attempt to make explicit the heuristic and control strategies employed.

Coaching – the teacher observes the students carrying out the task while offering feedback and prompts to bring their performance closer to that of an expert.

Scaffolding – the teacher provides support to the student while carrying out the task. This could take the form of suggestions, written materials, or actually carrying out part of the task for them. This idea obviously derives from the Vygotskyian concept of the zone of proximal development discussed earlier.

Articulation – this includes any techniques for getting the student to make explicit their knowledge and reasoning employed in the task.

Reflection – the teacher provides opportunities for students to compare their own processes with those of the teacher, their peers and ultimately their internal model of expert performance.

Exploration – techniques to make the students more autonomous, by forcing them into problem solving on their own. By the fading of support both for problem solving and for problem setting, the aim is to enable students to develop their skills of question setting and investigation.

Having decided on relevant teaching methods to achieve the required ends, the model next proposes three guiding principles for sequencing learning activities:

Practise global skills before local skills – by this means students develop a model for the whole process involved in the particular task, which will aid them in deciding on control strategies for carrying it out. This may require scaffolding for the parts of the task they cannot yet perform.

Increasing complexity – tasks should require an increasing level of domain knowledge, with a possible need for scaffolding which then fades away.

Increasing diversity – a wider variety of strategies and skills should need to be employed.

The final dimension is that of the social context for the learning. The model proposes that the following are characteristics of a social context that encourage positive beliefs about the nature of learning, and motivation and a positive approach to learning tasks:

Situated learning – this calls for realistic learning tasks in multiple contexts. It should enable students to see a purpose to their learning, be able to tell when it is appropriate to apply it, induce abstraction of the concepts, and encourage the possibility of transfer to other contexts.

Community of practice – this consists of opportunities for communication about different ways to accomplish tasks. It will be encouraged by common projects and shared experiences.

Intrinsic motivation – we have already discussed the important role this can play in our discussion of deep and surface approaches to learning. This can be strengthened by encouraging the setting of personal goals rather than by relying on reactions to external requirements.

Cooperation – this is encouraged by working together in groups, in pairs, in competition with other groups or not, as the situation demands.

RESEARCH TASK. COGNITIVE APPRENTICESHIP

Use the cognitive apprenticeship framework to develop some materials to accompany one of your courses.

Try to create resources in line with the ideas of modelling and scaffolding, that provide temporary support for the students while they develop more complex processes. These could include:

- making explicit and overt those procedures which are normally implicit;
- focusing attention on worthwhile alternatives by listing possible next steps;
- supplying hints, reminders and prompts;
- structuring procedures to encourage a deep approach to learning;
- structuring materials to encourage development of expert-like domain knowledge bases.

The aim is that when these supports are withdrawn, the student will be able to carry out the expert performance in their own right.

To investigate how successful this approach is, you may wish to adopt an observation schedule that will allow you to collect data on what the students do and say and ultimately assess whether they can carry out expert performance unaided.

(See Scardamalia et al., 1989, for a useful set of design principles for such materials. Although developed in the context of CAL materials many of the ideas are relevant whatever the type of resource.)

Pre-instructional strategies

Another interesting idea when considering the use of resource materials that presume a structure to the knowledge base and adopt a guided approach, is the adoption of pre-instructional strategies. Hartley and Davies (1976) discuss a number of ways of preparing students for learning tasks. Pre-tests are normally used to discover what prior knowledge students have of a topic so that new material can be keyed into what they already know. They are also used in tandem with post-tests to measure success of the learning process. However, they can also have a pre-instructional use in the sense that they alert students to what is to come, and sensitize them to what is deemed important. Another way of alerting students to what is to come is to present explicit objectives for a learning sequence. This can generate expectation and give some idea of what will be deemed evidence of achievement. A third way of introducing a course is to prepare an overview with summaries of what is to be covered, the central arguments, key concepts, general structure of the course, etc.

One pre-instructional strategy we wish to consider in more detail is the 'advance organizer', an idea suggested by Ausubel (1960). This is a conceptual framework that aims to clarify the learning task it precedes. It is usually prose, but could be visual (for instance a map, graph or network), explaining essential relationships in the forthcoming material. The aim is to help the learner fit new, more complex material into existing cognitive structures. The idea is becoming popular in CAL applications and in particular may have a role in hypermedia applications, which can become very confusing to learners as they tend not to have an obvious structure. Advance organizers may offer suggested pathways through the material and they can provide concept webs and navigation maps to present an outline of the material and highlight navigation routes for different goals (Hammond, 1989).

Advance organizers aim to aid learning in two ways. First they remind students of knowledge that they already possess that is relevant to the new knowledge that is to come, and secondly they prepare the learner for the new information by providing anchoring points for this new knowledge. These may seem obvious ideas but the traditional approach is to group homogeneous topics together and present them at a uniform conceptual level in a logical sequence depending on the development of the subject matter. You might like to prepare an advance organizer for part of a course. The aim would be to produce a substantive introduction to the material rather than the traditional historical introduction which places the content chronologically but not conceptually. Remember the following key points:

- the aim is to clarify the relationships within the material;
- the material should be at a higher level of abstraction and generality than the actual content to come;
- the content should be placed in context;

- the advance organizer should mobilize those relevant existing concepts which make the new knowledge more familiar and meaningful, and enable it to be utilized in the most effective way.

Having put the ideas of the whole learning environment into a theoretical framework, we now concentrate on two facets of assessing that environment: the teaching and learning issues of using a combination of resources and the organization and management of those resources.

Evaluation of the Resource Environment: Conversational Framework

A different approach to evaluating the resources that go to make up the learning environment is taken by Laurillard (1993). In the discussion of the generation of a general teaching strategy, the approach of phenomenography is preferred to that of instructional psychology, on the grounds that the latter does not go far enough towards prescribing a general description for a teaching strategy valid in all contexts. It concentrates on the difference between expert and novice performance but it does not describe how to get from one to the other, and although describing teaching strategies for particular contexts, such as the cognitive apprenticeship model, it is argued that it does not adequately explain how these can be generated from an empirical base.

Phenomenography, it is argued, provides descriptions of the internal structures of expert and novice conceptions, and clarifies what aspects of the conceptions should be focused on in the interaction between student and teacher. Learning is viewed as a conversation (see for example Pask, 1976 for a formal definition of conversation theory). 'The learning process must be constituted as a dialogue between teacher and student, operating at the level of descriptions of actions in the world, recognising the second-order character of academic knowledge' (Laurillard, 1993, p.94).

Taking this approach, Laurillard defines a 'conversational framework' as a specification of what is needed in a complete learning situation. Four categories are defined (here presented in a simplified form to give a flavour of the approach; for more detail see Laurillard, 1993):

Discursive – both teacher and student can describe their conceptions and modify their descriptions, in a recursive fashion, in the light of feedback and observation. Topic and task goals are negotiable.

Interactive – the teacher can set the task goal and the student can act to achieve it. Intrinsic feedback is given on the student's actions.

Adaptive – the teacher can adapt the task goal and the student can adapt their actions as the dialogue develops.

Reflective – the student can reflect on the feedback on their actions and link it to the topic goal, ie, can relate experience to the description of experience.

This framework can then be used to evaluate and classify educational media and resources. As a technique for analysing media generically it illuminates where a particular medium fails and what it might be combined with to fill the gap, thus giving indications on how to integrate a range of media to best advantage.

RESEARCH TASK. ANALYSIS OF RESOURCES USING CONVERSATIONAL FRAMEWORK

Assemble the complete range of materials you provide for a given course. Analyse them under the four headings of the conversational framework. For example:

- basic print materials on their own come only into the discursive category and then allow only the teacher to describe their conception; there is no possibility of modification;
- hypertext on its own has no specific goal for a student and gives no intrinsic feedback, so cannot be interactive, adaptive nor reflective. It does allow the teacher to describe their conception, and the student to describe and modify their conception by creating links;
- a computer microworld is completely interactive and allows the student to describe their conception, adapt their actions in the light of feedback and reflect on the feedback at leisure.

Identify any missing elements and see how additional material could be combined with existing material to fill the gap.

Assessing the Quality of Provision of Resources

Much of the discussion in the book so far, and the research tasks suggested, have concentrated on ways of providing a quality learning experience for the students through analysing educational and organizational goals and finding the most effective ways of reaching them.

Effective management of learning resources relies on strategic planning. Morgan (1995) provides a very up-to-date discussion of the issues, particularly of performance assessment, as well as providing a review of other recent publications in this field.

It is possible to count the numbers of books on the shelf, the amount of study space or professional librarians per student, the financial inputs and the effectiveness of processes such as the speed of inter-library loans, but it is far more difficult to measure effective learning outcomes. Surveys of student opinion would certainly suggest that students rate services such as libraries as very important to them. Some might argue that to assess the effect of the quality of resources provision upon learning outcomes is so difficult it would be better to concentrate on those more tangible aspects which can be measured and just to assume through the application of common sense that quality resources must be beneficial. You might like to explore how you, as a teacher, are placed to investigate the ways resource provision affects students' learning outcomes.

In the UK, a systematic set of performance indicators have been developed by the relevant funding councils (see Joint Funding Council, 1995) following recommendations contained in the Follett report (1993). Amongst the recommendations was the suggestion that performance indicators should be much more concerned with outputs than in the past. It is also significant, for academic staff, that one recommendation was that, 'the effectiveness of library and information services provision should be an important aspect in the assessment of the quality of teaching' (Follett, 1993, p.31).

The following research task uses the performance indicators developed after the Follett recommendations to assess the quality of resource provision within an institution. Other academics might well find your experience of this process interesting.

RESEARCH TASK. AN EVALUATION OF RESOURCE SERVICES THROUGH THE USE OF PERFORMANCE INDICATORS

Keep a record of your experience of collecting the following information in the form of a diary. Assemble data, either for your institution as a whole, or for your own department in cooperation with resources staff:

- *Integration:* how far are the objectives of resource services linked to institutional objectives? Particularly, what evidence is there to show the effective integration of the library service into the teaching, learning and research planning and review system? What are the feedback mechanisms between academic departments and resource providers? How are financial allocations decided?

- *User satisfaction:* what evidence is there that users are satisfied with support for their courses and research in terms of supply of resources, study facilities, information services and information skills tuition?
- *Delivery:* relate outputs to service and development targets including documents delivered, enquiries answered, information skills instruction, library study hours and volumes in stock per student.
- *Efficiency* (and value for money): how much service is provided in relation to the resource input? Indicators considered could include: items processed per member of staff and total expenditure per item processed; documents delivered per member of staff and total expenditure per document delivered; enquiries answered per member of staff and total expenditure per enquiry answered; total expenditure per study hour, volume in stock per member of staff and total expenditure per volume in stock.
- *Economy:* this relates inputs to clientele, including such items as library staff expenditure and operating costs, space, and acquisition costs.

Having compiled this data you may wish to consider the following:

- How useful do you feel the exercise was? Was it worth the time invested? What have you learnt?
- Do you feel that these indicators are appropriate in being versatile in application across institutions, as well as providing generic indicators to permit comparison across institutions? Can you suggest more appropriate indicators?

A much fuller account of this approach can be found in Joint Funding Council (1995).

Total Quality Management and Quality Standards

Two models emphasizing the importance of quality issues in management have been taken from commercial organizations and applied to educational services. They are Total Quality Management (TQM) and quality assurance. In the UK, BS 5750 has been the standard for quality assurance systems (now superseded by ISO 9000). Neither of these were evolved specifically for resource provision but both have been applied in that context. Freeman (1993) provides a detailed analysis of BS 5750 adapted for use in an educational context. He also provides a comparison between TQM and quality assurance. You might consider how useful these approaches would be in your own practice, either by full implementation or by selecting elements of them from this summary (adapted from Freeman, 1993, p.163ff):

Quality assurance is basically a management system. Its essential features are:

- a mission statement;
- a set of procedures which lay down how work shall be carried out;
- an auditing system to check compliance with procedures;
- a corrective action system to rectify non-compliance;
- a management review system to monitor and develop the system.

The thinking behind a quality assurance system maintains that:

- quality standards are derived from the customers' requirements;
- once established, if staff work to defined systems, those quality standards will be met;
- while staff help establish standards and write procedures, quality assurance systems are more about compliance than initiative.

Total Quality Management is essentially a system in which:

- every employee is enjoined to make continuous efforts towards continuous improvement;
- quality is measured more or less continuously by staff, small groups of staff act immediately on any problems which they identify;
- work methods are adjusted daily by small groups of staff in an effort to find ever more cost effective ways of achieving ever increasing quality.

The thinking behind a TQM system maintains that:

- quality standards should be improved all the time;
- once established, a standard is there to be bettered;
- all staff are under an obligation to identify problems and to share in finding solutions.

In his conclusion, Freeman suggests that there is insufficient evidence to conclude which approach is more usefully applied in the educational context. The quality assurance model could be seen as standardizing services rather than encouraging improvements. Total Quality Management encourages participation in the service at all levels and the delegation of authority to those in front-line services. Both approaches can be very time-consuming. Laurillard writes:

It is ironic that although higher education in the UK, for example, has a worldwide reputation for quality, it is being asked to borrow the inferior mechanisms of British management, which has an unenviably poor reputation worldwide. (Laurillard, 1993, p.224)

To what extent do you feel it could be appropriate to adopt techniques from commercial management in the pursuit of efficiency in the face of steadily increasing pressure from funding bodies?

Summary

This chapter, and the ones before, have inevitably been involved with assessment because to research learning resources requires consideration of their purpose and application. Approaches to resources can vary considerably and there are specific audiences to address.

Individual assessment of resources by staff is inevitable; for students it may well have to be directed. Group assessment of resources by staff and/or students can lead to different criteria emerging for consideration. Whole-class assessment will widen the perspective still further, as well as complicating the analysis of data and findings.

Course assessment of resources will involve a broader departmental view, which in turn may feed into a faculty understanding of resource provision. The overall institutional context, as managed and directed by an executive, will certainly have its more global vision of requirements, and this may involve discussing with and taking the views of outside bodies, perhaps governmental or to do with validation.

This can all lead to confusions, misunderstanding and undue complexity. Even so the use of resources is ongoing and therefore so is formative assessment of them. As a lecturer you have to use the material available, lobby for more wherever possible, and often create your own along the way. This being the case, you have a vested interest for your students' sake in making the best use of what is available, and being able to argue positively for more, based on empirical research. Where there are gaps in resource provision, see if you can fill them through your flexibility and versatility, through adjusting and modifying your practice.

It is worth reiterating here that ideally you are the prime resource because your experience, commitment and skill can be channelled down many routes, whereas the physical resources you use, whether old or new, remain merely the vehicle for your desire to meet your students' needs. There is an old saying that some people cannot see the wood for the trees, and with resources you do certainly need to think laterally so that the wealth of potential and actual resources are open to view and so that you do not become set in seeing learning resources as a fixed, finite or limited set of material.

Annotated Reading List

Laurillard, D (1993) *Rethinking University Teaching: A framework for the effective use of educational technology*, London: Routledge.
A very comprehensive book which develops a practical methodology for the design, development and implementation of educational technologies; it compares and evaluates the current media and teaching methods.

Marton, F, Hounsell, D and Entwistle, E (eds) (1984) *The Experience of Learning*, Edinburgh: Scottish Academic Press.
A fascinating collection of essays on how students learn in higher education. Useful for the insights of the essays and for the discussion of the research methodologies employed.

Morgan, S (1995) Performance Assessment in Academic Libraries, London: Mansell.
Discussion of the issues and a review of recent publications in this field.

Ramsden, P (1992) *Learning to Teach in Higher Education*, London: Routledge.
An interesting book linking educational theory with the practicalities of teaching in higher education.

References

Ausubel, D P (1960) 'The use of advance organizers in the learning and retention of meaningful verbal material', *Journal of Educational Psychology*, 51, 5, 267–72.

Collins, A, Brown, J S and Newman, S (1989) 'Cognitive apprenticeship: teaching the craft of reading, writing and mathematics', in Resnick, L B (ed.) *Knowing, Learning and Instruction: Essays in Honor of Robert Glaser*, Hillsdale, NJ: Lawrence Erlbaum Associates.

Collins, A, Brown, J S and Holum, A (1991) 'Cognitive apprenticeship: making thinking visible', *American Educator*, 15, 3, 6–11, 38–46.

De Corte, E (1990) 'Learning with new information technologies in schools: perspectives from the psychology of learning and instruction', *Journal of Computer Assisted Learning*, 6, 69–87.

Entwistle, N J (1981) *Styles of Learning and Teaching: An integrated outline of educational psychology for students, teachers and lecturers*, New York: John Wiley.

Entwistle, N J and Ramsden, P (1983) *Understanding Student Learning*, Beckenham: Croom Helm.

Follett, B (Chairman) (1993) *Joint Funding Council's Libraries Review Group: Report*, Bristol: Higher Education Funding Council for England.

Fransson, A (1977) 'On qualitative differences in learning IV: Effects of motivation and test anxiety on process and outcome', *British Journal of Educational Psychology*, 47, 244–57.

Freeman, R (1993) *Quality Assurance in Training and Education: How to apply BS 5750 (ISO 9000) Standards*, London: Kogan Page.

Hammond, N (1989) 'Hypermedia and learning: who guides whom?', in Maurer, H (ed.) *Computer-assisted Learning, proceedings of Second International Conference ICCAL 1989*, Berlin: Springer-Verlag.

Hartley, J and Davies, I K (1976) 'Pre instructional strategies: the role of pretests, behavioural objectives, overviews and advance organizers', *Review of Educational Research*, 46, 2, 239–65.

Joint Funding Councils' Ad Hoc Group on Performance Indicators for Libraries (1995) *The Effective Academic Library: A framework for evaluating the performance of UK academic libraries*, Bristol: HEFCE.

Laurillard, D (1993) *Rethinking University Teaching: A framework for the effective use of educational technology*, London: Routledge.

Marton, F and Säljö, R (1976a) 'On qualitative differences in learning I: outcome and process', *British Journal of Educational Psychology*, 46, 4–11.

Marton, F and Säljö, R (1976b) 'On qualitative differences in learning II: outcome as a function of the learner's conception of the task', *British Journal of Educational Psychology*, 46, 115–27.

Marton, F and Säljö, R (1984) 'Approaches to learning', in Marton, F, Hounsell, D and Entwistle, E (eds) (1984) *The Experience of Learning*, Edinburgh: Scottish Academic Press.

Morgan, S (1995) *Performance Assessment in Academic Libraries*, London: Mansell.

Palincsar, A S and Brown, A L (1984) 'Reciprocal teaching of comprehension-fostering and monitoring activities', *Cognition and Instruction*, 1, 117–75.

Pask, G (1976) 'Conversational techniques in the study and practice of education', *British Journal of Educational Psychology*, 46, 12–25.

Polya, G (1945) *How to Solve It*, Princeton, NJ: Princeton University Press.

Ramsden, P (1992) *Learning to Teach in Higher Education*, London: Routledge.

Resnick, L B (1983) 'Toward a cognitive theory of instruction', in Paris, S G, Olson, G M and Stevenson, H W (eds) *Learning and Motivation in the Classroom*, Hillsdale, NJ: Lawrence Erlbaum Associates.

Säljö, R (1975) *Qualitative Differences in Learning as a Function of the Learner's Conception of the Task*, Gothenburg: Acta Universitatis Gothoburgensis.

Säljö, R (1979) *Learning in the learner's perspective: Some common sense conceptions*, Reports from the Institute of Education 76, University of Gothenberg.

Scardamalia, M and Bereiter, C (1985) 'Fostering the development of self-regulation in children's knowledge processing', in Chipman, S F, Segal, J W and Glaser, R (eds) *Thinking and Learning Skills: Research and open questions*, Hillsdale, NJ: Lawrence Erlbaum Associates.

Scardamalia, M, Bereiter, C, McLean, R, Swallow, J and Woodruff, E (1989) 'Computer-supported intentional learning environments', *Journal of Educational Computing Research*, 5, 51–68.

Schoenfeld, A H (1985) *Mathematical Problem Solving*, New York: Academic Press.

Svensson, L (1977) 'On qualitative differences in learning III: Study skill and learning', *British Journal of Educational Psychology*, 47, 233–43.

Van Rossum, E J and Schenk, S M (1984) 'The relationship between learning conception, study strategy and learning outcome', *British Journal of Educational Psychology*, 54, 73–83.

Chapter 7

Series Conclusion: Getting Published

Kate Ashcroft

Getting started on writing a book is often the hardest part of the process. You need to convince yourself that the things that you know about and that interest you will matter sufficiently to other people to make publication worthwhile, and then you have to get down to it. In choosing a topic for a book, there is always a balance to be struck between your needs and those of the reader. For example, you may have completed a research degree in the area of student interaction with learning materials, and found the subject of your dissertation interesting. However, it is likely to require a complete rewrite and reorientation of the way you approach the subject before it becomes interesting to a larger group of readers.

Publishers receive much unsolicited material through the mail, often in the form of a covering letter and some 'finished' material. Most will consider such approaches carefully. Even so, this is likely to be the least productive way of approaching a publisher. The highest 'hit' rate is likely to be achieved if you are invited to put a proposal forward. Such invitations do not happen by accident. They often result from putting yourself in the right place at the right time. To do this, you may need to develop networks of contacts. Commissioning editors get to know about potential authors through a number of routes. They attend conferences: you can meet them there and talk to them about your specialist area. They ask influential groups and individuals about likely authors when they perceive a niche in the market: you might get to know the committee members of relevant associations and make sure they know about your potential contribution. They often ask established writers to contribute to book series. These 'names' often have sufficient commissions already. If you can get to know established authors, and ensure that they know about you and your interests, they may suggest your name to the editor instead. Commissioning editors also read the educational press, not so much learned journals as papers such as *The Times Educational Supplement, The Times Higher Educational Supplement* and *Education*. If you have written for such papers, your name may become known in the right circles.

Editors also look for pockets of good practice and investigate them for potential authors. If your institution has had an excellent inspection report, or if you are a member of a consortium of colleges or universities that share good practice, you do not have to wait to be discovered. It may be worth drawing an editor's attention to what you are doing and to invite them to talk to you and others about its publishing potential.

I have to admit to never having acted in the ways described above. I received commissions the hard way: by putting a good quality submission to an appropriate publisher. I have been successful when I looked at the process from the editor's point of view. The publisher is much more interested in their readers' needs, and in making a profit, than in your interests. If you can present what you want to do in these terms, you may be successful. This is likely to require some research to find out who your readers are likely to be, how many of them there are, where they will be found, what their interests are and why they will want to buy your particular book.

The publisher will also be interested in the competition for the book you are proposing. If you tell them there is no competition, you are likely to be asked to do more research. If you still cannot find books on your subject, the publisher may worry that there is a good reason why nobody else is publishing in that area. You may be more successful if you undertake a thorough trawl of other publications on topics related to the one that you wish to write about, and then think clearly about your particular selling points and how you can make your book better than the others on the market. Your arguments may vary, depending on what you are writing about. When I co-edited a book on the new National Curriculum, we pointed out that it would be particularly timely (it was to be the first book after the new Orders were published). When I wrote a book on quality and standards, I made sure that it looked at quality issues from the lecturer's point of view (others mainly wrote for institutional managers).

Choosing a Publisher

Once you are clear about what you intend to write and who you are writing for, you will need to choose a publisher. In the UK, there are a relatively small number of publishing houses that specialize in books about education and that are interested in publishing material about further and higher education in particular. Most of the main ones feature in the annotated list of publishers towards the end of this chapter. In addition, there are a number of publishers who are based in other countries, and some universities have developed their own small in-house publishing companies.

A few academic authors use a literary agent. If you wish to do so, the *Writers' and Artists' Yearbook* will help you locate one. The agent will place your book with an appropriate publisher, do most of the negotiation on your behalf, act as a critical friend, take care of the bookkeeping, correspondence and so on. The academic book market works with low profit margins. For this reason royalty schemes are fairly inflexible. Once you have paid their fees, using a literary agent is unlikely make you much more money.

If you decide to go it alone, you may find it useful to look around at the book lists of various publishers to find those that have a sizeable list in your subject. It is easier to market a group of books with a common theme. You will also have to decide whether to go for a large publishing house or a smaller, more specialized one. Larger houses have the marketing facilities to promote books across the world. On the other hand, junior editors in large houses have little power and may take some time to get approval for action. Small publishing houses may give more personal service. They also tend to be more highly specialized and so know a lot about publishing in a particular field.

If you are new to writing for publication, it is probably worth phoning likely publishing houses to talk to the commissioning editor for post-compulsory education or making contact with publishing representatives at conferences. You can then talk about your ideas to see if he or she is interested in them. Generally, the commissioning editor will be happy to provide you with guidelines on how to submit a formal proposal. Provided you let them know you are doing so, publishers generally do not object if you put your book outline to two or three houses.

If the commissioning editor likes your proposal, they will usually ask for reports from a couple of referees. The referees' reports often contain suggestions for change. Try not be discouraged by this. It is not at all unusual to be asked for clarification, more information or slight changes before a proposal is accepted. This process can improve the proposal considerably.

Negotiating the Contract

Once it looks like you are more or less 'in business', you will need to discuss terms and conditions. The level of royalties offered by academic publishers does not vary greatly, but it is always worth trying to negotiate a slightly better deal or asking for a small advance on royalties, especially if you are involved in some immediate expenses (for instance, a new computer or photographic material). Whatever terms you eventually agree, it is important to read your contract carefully. Most are fairly standard. You may be paid royalties as a percentage of the net price. On the other hand, especially if your book is the type that may be sold at a discount (for instance, through book clubs), your royalties may be a percentage of net receipts (what the publishing house actually receives from sales). This arrangement allows the publisher to pay you a lower amount per book sold, where the books are sold at a discount. If you are editing a book with chapters contributed by others, the publishing house may pay the chapter authors a small fee on publication. The total of these fees may then be set against your royalties.

Copyright may be held by the publisher or the author. In practice, this may make little difference, as in any case the publisher will normally reserve exclusive publishing rights. In other cases the small print on contracts can be important. For instance, I would never sign a contract that gave the publisher an option on subsequent books.

Your contract is likely to say that the publisher reserves the right not to publish your book if your deliver it after a fixed date or if it is of poor quality. In practice, these clauses are not often invoked, but you should not rely on this, as such slippage often causes the editor difficulties and may make it less likely that he or she will look favourably on your next proposal. If your book does not come up to expectations, he or she will also usually help you to improve it, rather than abandon it altogether.

It is in your interests to undertake careful proof-reading at the early stages. Once the book has been typeset, substantial changes late in the process can have knock-on effects you may not have anticipated: for instance, the indexing may need to be redone. There will usually be a clause in the contract about excess correction charges that could be expensive for you. Do not forget to check the spelling on the title pages. I have heard of a spelling mistake that was found on the cover after binding; the book had to be reprinted and as a consequence the author lost several hundred pounds in royalties.

One decision you will have to make is whether to do your own indexing. Most publishers have links with professional indexers who will do this job for you for a charge that is set against royalties. Professional indexers usually do a sound job, but they may not know the subject area as well as you do. If you decide to do your own index, your editor should be able to provide you with guidelines on the house style and give you tips to make the job relatively painless (for instance, using a highlighter on a photocopy at the proof-reading stage to mark significant words and phrases). There are indexing computer programs that can simplify the job a little.

Many authors stick with one editor for a considerable time. This relationship will be much easier if you are the sort of person who meets deadlines. Your editor is more likely to work hard on behalf of a cooperative and efficient author who answers correspondence promptly and delivers on time. Because the unexpected always occurs, I aim to complete the book well before the agreed deadline.

Good time management requires planning from the start. It may be useful to audit your position, to look at your commitments and decide what it is possible to do and to allow some leeway in the schedule. I am always disconcerted by the amount of time finishing a book takes (checking references, tidying headings, creating the table of contents and so on). When you submit the manuscript, you need to be prepared for more work. The publisher may send you a marked-up manuscript to check before typesetting. If so, it is important that you have set aside the time to do a thorough job. This will be the last chance to make substantive changes. After the manuscript has been typeset, you may be asked to undertake thorough and careful proof-reading. At the same time, it is likely that you will be approached by the marketing department with requests for a range of information to help the publisher to sell the book. This is an important stage, and one to which you should give time and thought. It is probably a good idea to talk through the post-submission schedule with your publisher, so that you can blank out some days in your diary to do all this work.

The marketing of your book is partially your responsibility. The low profit margin on academic books means that your book is unlikely to be advertised in the press (unless it is part of a series that may be included in a composite advertisement). A few books will be sent out for review. If you expect to see your book described in the educational press during the following months, you may be disappointed. Not all books sent for review will be included and, even where they are, the review may not be printed for up to a year. Much marketing takes place through direct mail shots. The publicity department will need your help in targeting these. Another important marketing outlet is the conference circuit. You will need to inform the marketing department of key events where publicity about your book should be available. If you are giving a paper at a conference, you should make sure that your book is on prominent display. Do not be afraid to act as a shameless self-publicist.

Writing for a Journal

The most usual way of getting started in publishing is to write for a newspaper or journal. If you submit articles to the educational press, you will be up against stiff competition from professional journalists. Unless you have already established a name within education, you may find it is a difficult field to break into. You may be more likely to succeed if your article has something special that will catch the editor's attention. This 'something' may be topicality, controversy or human interest. If your area of enquiry has started to feature as a national issue (for example, the effects of cut backs in resources on the quality of students' learning), it is worth submitting a timely article to the educational press. If what you want to say is of direct application or relevance to the reader (for instance, a resource-centred teaching technique that has direct classroom application), it may be publishable. The educational press prefers interesting articles, written in a short and non-technical way. It may not be interested in straightforward research reports.

Journals are likely to be more interested in the sort of research and enquiry that we have been suggesting in this series. You are unlikely to be paid for a paper or article in a journal, but this form of publishing can make a good starting point for a would-be academic author. Once you have completed your thinking, reading, research and/or enquiry, ideally you should start to consider the journals that might accept it before you start writing so that you can adapt your style to their requirements.

On the whole, you will achieve more status and professional recognition if you publish in a refereed journal, especially if it reaches an international audience. The refereeing process means that the quality of your paper is subjected to scrutiny by (usually two) outside experts, before it is published. They will often suggest that you should change your paper in various ways. You may want to consider these requests very seriously, since they are usually made by people who know a great deal about the subject and about writing. On the other hand, the paper is yours, and you may decide not to agree to changes if that would make the paper say things that you disagree with or change the tone you wish to take.

More status is accorded to publication in very well established journals. On the other hand, they tend to have a large number of experienced writers who regularly write for them: your paper will compete for space with many experts. You may stand a better chance of being published if you submit to a relatively new publication. My first paper appeared in the (then) new international journal *Assessment and Evaluation in Higher Education* that has now grown into a very well respected publication. If you start with a new journal, and if you both do well, you can build a long-lasting relationship to your mutual benefit.

The frequency of publication may be another factor in your choice of journal. Journals that only appear once or twice a year may not deal with your paper expeditiously. Since it is generally not 'done' to send your paper to several journals at the same time, this can be a real problem. A journal that publishes more regularly will probably referee and publish your paper more quickly. This is especially important if your paper is on a topical theme.

You will find detailed guidance at the back of most journals on how to set out your manuscript, references and so on. It will generally explain the usual length of acceptable articles and the number of copies of the manuscript that must be sent. It is important to keep to these guidelines.

Finding your Voice

When you start writing you will need to find your own style. On the whole it may be better for inexperienced writers to keep their style serious but simple. It is tempting to try to sound more authoritative by a 'mock posh' or passive way of writing. This is usually a mistake. Straightforward reporting, using as little jargon and as few conditional clauses as is consistent with the complexity of your subject matter, will probably work best.

The unique selling point of your book will influence the register and style of your writing. If you are writing for a highly specialized readership, with a wealth of expert knowledge and experience of reading difficult texts, you may get away with a more dense and complex writing style. On the other hand, if you are writing for students, or busy lecturers or teachers, simple English with short sentences and paragraphs may communicate better. Avoid being pompous but remember that books are different from letters and newspaper articles, and need a slightly more formal style. 'Conversational' styles of writing can come across as patronizing or unintelligent. For this reason, it is hard to bring off jokes or rhetorical questions in academic writing.

Gradually, you should learn to recognize your strengths and weaknesses. This awareness builds painfully over time. Ask friends or colleagues to read through anything you submit for publication and to be as critical and demanding as possible. Be prepared to rewrite if necessary.

Education Publishers

Below I have listed many of the major publishers which are interested in books and/or curriculum materials to support teaching and learning within colleges and universities.

Cassell, Villiers House, 41/47 Strand, London WC2N 5JE. Telephone: 0171 420 5555.
Cassell publishes books aimed at teachers and undergraduate and postgraduate students of education and at the general market. The books reflect the most recent research into education, psychology and related academic subjects. While being at the cutting edge, they should also be clearly written and accessible. They are frequently aimed at the international market, while covering the most up-to-date policy developments in the UK.

David Fulton, 2 Barbon Close, Great Ormond Street, London WC1N 3JX. Telephone: 0171 405 5656.
David Fulton specializes in publishing within education, with a focus towards teachers of students and children with profound and multiple learning difficulties. It also publishes much for initial teacher education. It wishes to build from this very strong base a list that covers other issues in the college and university sector.
It mainly publishes books which, while grounded in current research or classroom practice, set out lessons and issues for people to use in their professional practice or in their studies. It does not publish research *per se*, nor publish exclusively for the academic community. It is a good publishing firm for a new author, since it will provide a personal service that includes much support and encouragement.

Falmer Press, 27 Palmeira Mansions, Church Road, Hove, East Sussex BN3 2FA Telephone: 01273 775154.
Falmer is a large and prestigious educational publisher. Once it has accepted your proposal, if you are an experienced author it will allow you to get on with your writing with little interference. This has the advantage of allowing much freedom, but does require that you are disciplined and know what you are doing.
Its list covers a wide variety of age ranges and subjects within education, including books on adolescence, equal opportunities, curriculum, educational policy and management, the disciplines of

education, subject teaching, teacher education and student learning. The books are authoritative and well researched. They are aimed at students, practitioners and academics.

Framework Press, Parkfield, Greaves Road, Lancaster LA1 4TZ. Telephone: 01524 39602.
This is a small, specialist publisher that is particularly interested in interactive curriculum and development materials. Much of its output is in the form of student-centred, activity-based material, in a ring-bound, photocopiable format (although it occasionally publishes books). The audience that it caters for includes students, teachers and educational managers. The list covers school and college management; staff development within schools, colleges and universities; vocational material, especially related to GNVQ; and curriculum material for English and Personal Social Education. The commissioning editor is interested in material covering all aspects of assessment and evaluation. If you are thinking of creating materials that will allow your readership to interact and to do things, rather than to take away and read, this may be the outlet for you.

Further Education Development Agency, Publications Department, Coombe Lodge, Blagdon, Bristol BS18 6RG. Telephone: 01761 462503.
This new agency is developing a publication list that will cover a variety of aspects of teaching, learning, assessment and management, focusing particularly on the further education sector.

Heinemann, Halley Court, Jordan Hill, Oxford OX2 8EJ. Telephone: 01865 311366.
Heinemann is one of the major educational publishers. Its list covers a wide variety of aspects of teaching, learning, assessment and management in both the university and college sector.

Hodder and Stoughton, 338 Euston Road, London NW1 3BH. Telephone: 0171 873 6000.
Hodder and Stoughton Educational covers a wide range of subjects for further and higher education, including business, health and caring, catering, beauty therapy and vocational languages. At the higher education level, it has a teacher education list with a strongly practical focus, some of which is published in cooperation with the Open University.
Most of its publishing is taken up with core and supplementary textbooks, supported by teacher packs and student-centred workbooks. Its language publishing is fully supported by audio packs, with prize-winning CD-ROMs accompanying some courses.

Jessica Kingsley, 116 Pentonville Road, London N1 9JB. Telephone: 0171 833 2307.
Jessica Kingsley publishes books mainly for professionals. It asks authors to bear in mind that the essence of the sort of publishing it does is that is a combination of theory and practice.

Journal of Information Technology for Teacher Education
    Triangle. Published three times a year.
    Manuscripts to: B Robinson, Department of Education, University of
    Cambridge, 17 Trumpington Street, Cambridge CB2 1QA.
    This well-established international, refereed journal is concerned with all
    aspects of information technology within pre- and inservice teacher
    education. In general, the papers are rather oriented to schools and
    university teacher education departments, but if you have undertaken a
    staff or course development project involving technology, you might find
    this is a useful outlet. The tone of the papers varies from reader-friendly
    to highly technical. The scope of many of the papers is limited and
    includes some insider research reports.

Journal of Open and Distance Learning
    Open University/Pitman. Published three times a year.
    Manuscripts to: J Matthews, Regional Academic Services, The Open
    University, Walton Hall, Milton Keynes MK7 6AA.
    This international refereed journal covers any aspects of open or distance
    learning. It publishes long articles and shorter pieces that include surveys,
    conceptual pieces, debates of current issues and research reports. It is
    primarily concerned with post-compulsory education. The style and topics
    are very varied.

Learning Resources Journal
    Learning Resources Development Group. Published three times a year.
    Manuscripts to: D Bosworth, Malford Grove, Gilvern, Abergavenny, Gwent
    NP7 0RN.
    This journal covers any aspect of the preparation, management,
    organization or retrieval of learning resources. The papers include
    reports of case studies, research projects and surveys. The articles are
    highly eclectic and most are short and written in user-friendly language.

Other education-related journals

You may be interested in publishing in some of the journals listed below.
The editorial policy of some of them are described in Ashcroft and Palacio
(1996), Ashcroft *et al.* (1996), Bennett *et al.* (1996) or Jones *et al.* (1996).

Applied Behavioural Science Review
    JAI Press Inc. Published twice a year.
    Manuscripts to: D W Britt, Wayne State University, USA.
Assessment and Evaluation in Higher Education
    Carfax. Published three times a year.
    Manuscripts to: W A H Scott, School of Education, University of Bath.
Assessment in Education: Principles, Policy and Practice
    Carfax. Published three times a year.
    Manuscripts to: P Broadfoot, School of Education, University of Bristol.

Association for Learning Technology Journal
Association for Learning Technology. Published twice a year.
Manuscripts to: G Jacob, University College, Swansea.

British Educational Research Journal
Carfax. Published quarterly.
Manuscripts to: G Weiner, Department of Education, South Bank
Polytechnic, London.

British Journal of Educational Psychology
British Psychological Society. Published quarterly.
Manuscripts to: M Youngman, School of Education, University of
Nottingham, University Park, Nottingham.

British Journal of Educational Studies
Blackwell. Published quarterly.
Manuscripts to: D Halpin, Institute of Education, University of Warwick,
Coventry.

British Journal of In-Service Education
Triangle. Published three times a year.
Manuscripts to: M Lee, University College of Bretton Hall, Wakefield.

British Journal of Music Education
Cambridge University Press. Published three times a year.
Manuscripts to: J Paynter, University of York, or K Swanwick, University of
London Institute of Education.

British Journal of Religious Education
Alden Press. Published three times a year.
Manuscripts to: J M Hall, University of Birmingham.

British Journal of Sociology of Education
Carfax. Published quarterly.
Manuscripts to: L Barton, Division of Education, University of Sheffield.

Cambridge Journal of Education
Triangle. Published three times a year.
Manuscripts to: B Shannon, University of Cambridge Institute of
Education.

Comparative Education
Carfax, three times a year.
Manuscripts to: P Broadfoot, University of Bristol.

Compare: A Journal of Comparative Education
Carfax. Published three times a year.
Manuscripts to: C Brock, University of Oxford.

Computers and Education
Pergamon. Published eight times a year.
Manuscripts to: M R Kibby, University of Strathclyde.

Curriculum Inquiry
Blackwell. Published quarterly.
Manuscripts to: F M Connolly, The Ontario Institute for Studies in
Education, Canada.

The Curriculum Journal
　　Routledge. Published three times a year.
　　Manuscripts to: M James, University of Cambridge Institute of Education.
Curriculum Studies
　　Triangle. Published three times a year.
　　Manuscripts to: W Carr, Division of Education, University of Sheffield.
Disability and Society
　　Carfax. Published quarterly.
　　Manuscripts to: L Barton, Division of Education, University of Sheffield
Education Economics
　　Carfax. Published three times a year.
　　Manuscripts to: G Johnes, Lancaster University.
Education Today
　　Pitman. Published quarterly.
　　Manuscripts to: The Editor, College of Preceptors, Coppice Row,
　　Theydon Bois, Epping.
Educational Management and Administration
　　Pitman. Published quarterly.
　　Manuscripts to: P Ribbins, University of Birmingham.
Educational Action Research
　　Triangle. Published three times a year.
　　Manuscripts to: Dr B Somekh, University of East Anglia, Norwich.
Educational Psychology
　　Carfax. Published quarterly.
　　Manuscripts to: R Riding, University of Birmingham.
Educational Research
　　Routledge. Published three time a year.
　　Manuscripts to: S Hegarty, National Foundation for Educational
　　Research, Slough.
Educational Research and Evaluation
　　Swets and Zeitlinger. Published quarterly.
　　Manuscripts to: B P M Creemers, GION, University of Groningen, The
　　Netherlands.
Educational Review
　　Carfax. Published three times a year.
　　Manuscripts to: The Editors, School of Education, University of Birmingham.
Educational Studies
　　Carfax. Published three times a year.
　　Manuscripts to: D Cherrington, International Centre for Advanced
　　Studies, Cheltenham and Gloucester College of Higher Education.
Educational Studies in Mathematics
　　Kluwer Academic Publishers. Published four times a year.
　　Manuscripts to: Kluwer Academic Publishers, Dordrecht, The Netherlands.
Educational Theory
　　University of Illinois. Published four times a year.
　　Manuscripts to: N C Burbules, University of Illinois, USA.

Environmental Education Research
  Carfax. Published three times a year.
  Manuscripts to: C Oulton, University of Bath.
European Journal of Education
  Carfax. Published quarterly.
  Manuscripts to: The Editors, European Institute of Education and Social
  Policy, Université de Paris.
European Journal of Engineering Education
  Carfax, Published quarterly.
  Manuscripts to: T Becher, University of Sussex.
European Journal of Special Needs
  Routledge. Published three times a year.
  Manuscripts to: S Hegarty, National Foundation for Educational Research.
European Journal of Teacher Education
  Carfax. Published three times a year.
  Manuscripts to: M Todeschini, Istituto di Pedagogia, Universita degli
  studii, Milano, Italy.
Evaluation and Research in Education
  Multilingual Matters. Published three times a year.
  Manuscripts to: K Morrison, School of Education, University of Durham.
Evaluation Practice
  JAI Press. Published three times a year.
  Manuscripts to: M Smith, University of Maryland, USA.
Forum for Promoting 3–19 Comprehensive Education
  Triangle. Published three times a year.
  Manuscripts to: N Whitbread, Beaumont Cottage, East Langton, Market
  Harborough.
Gender and Education
  Carfax. Published three times a year.
  Manuscripts to: C Hughes, Department of Continuing Education,
  University of Warwick.
Higher Education Policy
  Kogan Page. Published quarterly.
  Manuscripts to: International Association of Universities, Paris, France.
Higher Education Quarterly
  Blackwells. Published quarterly.
  Manuscripts to: M Shattock, Senate House, University of Warwick.
Higher Education Review
  Tyrrell Burgess Associates. Published three times a year.
  Manuscripts to: J Pratt, 46 Merers Road, London.
*Innovation and Learning in Education: The International Journal for the Reflective
  Practitioner*
  MCB University Press. Published three times a year.
  Manuscripts to: G McElwee, School of Management, University of
  Humberside, Hull.

Innovations in Education and Training International
   Kogan Page. Published quarterly.
   Manuscripts to: C Bell, University of Plymouth.
Interchange
   Kluwer Academic Press. Published three times a year.
   Manuscripts to: L Lenz, Faculty of Education, University of Calgary,
   Canada.
International Journal of Disability and Development in Education
   University of Queensland Press. Published three times a year.
   Manuscripts to: F and E Schonell, Special Education Centre, St Lucia,
   Australia.
International Journal of Education Research
   Pergamon Press. Published 12 times a year.
   Manuscripts to: H J Walberg, University of Illinois, Chicago, USA.
International Journal of Science Education
   Taylor and Francis. Published six times a year.
   Manuscripts to: J K Gilbert, University of Reading.
International Journal of Technology and Design Education
   Kluwer Academic Press. Published three times a year.
   Manuscripts to: The Editor, Kluwer Academic Publishers, Dordrecht, The
   Netherlands.
International Research in Geographical and Environmental Education
   La Trobe University Press. Published twice a year.
   Manuscripts to: J Lidstone, Queensland University of Technology,
   Australia.
International Studies in Sociology of Education
   Triangle. Published twice a year.
   Manuscripts to: L Barton, Division of Education, University of Sheffield.
Issues in Education: Contributions from Educational Psychology
   JAI Press. Published twice a year.
   Manuscripts to: J Carson, School of Education, University of California, USA.
Journal for Educational Policy
   Taylor and Francis. Published six times a year.
   Manuscripts to: S Ball, Kings College, London.
Journal of Access Studies
   Jessica Kingsley, Published twice a year.
   Manuscripts to: P Jones, Higher Education Quality Council.
Journal of Aesthetic Education
   University of Illinois Press. Published quarterly.
   Manuscripts to: University of Illinois, USA.
Journal of Art and Design Education
   Blackwell. Published three times a year.
   Manuscripts to: J Swift, University of Central England, Birmingham.
Journal of Biological Education
   Institute of Biology. Published quarterly.
   Manuscripts to: The Editor, 20–22 Queensberry Place, London.

Journal of Computer Assisted Learning
Blackwell. Published quarterly.
Manuscripts to: R Lewis, University of Lancaster.
Journal of Education for Teaching
Carfax. Published three times a year.
Manuscripts to: E Stones, 11 Serpentine Road, Selly Park, Birmingham.
Journal of Educational Television
Carfax. Published three times a year.
Manuscripts to: M Messenger Davies, The London Institute.
Journal of Further and Higher Education
NATFHE. Published three times a year.
Manuscripts to: A Castling, c/o NATFHE, London.
Journal of Geography in Higher Education
Carfax. Published three times a year.
Manuscripts to: M Healey, Cheltenham and Gloucester College of Higher
Education.
Journal of Information Technology for Teacher Education
Triangle. Published three times a year.
Manuscripts to: B Robinson, Department of Education, University of
Cambridge.
Journal of Moral Education
Carfax. Published three times a year.
Manuscripts to: M J Taylor, National Foundation for Educational Research.
Journal of Open and Distance Learning
Open University/ Pitman. Published three times a year.
Manuscripts to: J Matthews, Regional Academic Services, The Open
University, Milton Keynes.
Journal of Philosophy of Education
Redwood Books. Published three times a year.
Manuscripts to: R Smith, University of Durham.
Journal of Teacher Development
Pitman. Published quarterly.
Manuscripts to: M Golby, School of Education, University of Exeter.
Learning and Individual Differences: A Multidisciplinary Journal of Education
JAI Press. Published quarterly.
Manuscripts to: F N Dempster, University of Nevada, Las Vegas, USA.
Management in Education
Pitman. Published quarterly.
Manuscripts to: The Editor, Putteridge Bury, University of Luton.
Medical Teacher
Carfax. Published quarterly.
Manuscripts to: R M Harden, Ninewells Hospital and Medical School.
Mentoring and Tutoring for Partnership in Learning
Trentham Books. Published three times a year.
Manuscripts to: J Egglestone, c/o Trentham Books, Stoke on Trent.

Multicultural Teaching to Combat Racism in School and Community
  Trentham Books. Published three times a year.
  Manuscripts to: G Klein, Department of Education, University of Warwick.
Pastoral Care in Education
  Blackwells. Published six times a year.
  Manuscripts to: R Best, Froebel Institute College, London.
New Academic
  SEDA. Published three times a year.
  Manuscripts to: E Mapstone, St Yse, St Nectan's Glen, Tintagel, Cornwall.
Oxford Review of Education
  Carfax. Published three times a year.
  Manuscripts to: D Phillips, University of Oxford Department of
  Educational Studies.
Physics Education
  Institute of Physics Publishing. Published three times a year.
  Manuscripts to: Institute of Physics, Bristol.
Qualitative Studies in Education
  Taylor and Francis. Published four times a year.
  Manuscripts to: S Ball, Centre for Educational Studies, King's College,
  London.
Quality Assurance in Education
  MCB University Press. Published three times a year.
  Manuscripts to: G McElwee, School of Management, University of
  Humberside, Hull.
Quality in Higher Education
  Carfax. Published three times a year.
  Manuscripts to: L Harvey, University of Central England, Birmingham.
Research in Drama Education
  Carfax. Published quarterly.
  Manuscripts to: J Somers, University of Exeter.
Research into Science and Technological Education
  Carfax. Published twice a year.
  Manuscripts to: C R Brown, University of Hull.
Research Papers in Education
  Routledge. Published three times a year.
  Manuscripts to: P Preece, School of Education, University of Exeter.
Sport, Education and Society
  Carfax. Published quarterly.
  Manuscripts to: C Hardy, University of Loughborough.
Studies in Educational Evaluation
  Pergamon. Published quarterly.
  Manuscripts to: A Lewy, School of Education, Tel Aviv University, Israel;
  M Alkin, Graduate School of Education, UCLA, USA; B McGaw,
  Australian Council of Educational Research, Victoria; or R Langeheine,
  Institute for Science Education (IPN), University of Kiel, Germany.

Studies in Higher Education
  Society for Research into Higher Education/Carfax. Published quarterly.
  Manuscripts to: R Barnett, Centre for Higher Education Studies, Institute
  of Education, London.
Teaching and Teacher Education
  Pergamon Press. Published six times a year.
  Manuscripts to: N Bennett, University of Exeter.
Teachers and Teaching: Theory and Practice
  Carfax. Published three times a year.
  Manuscripts to: C Day, ISATT, University of Nottingham.
  Teaching in Higher Education
  Carfax. Published three times a year.
  Manuscripts to: L Barton, Division of Education, University of Sheffield.
Tertiary Education and Management
  Jessica Kingsley. Published twice a year.
  Manuscripts to: N R Begg, The University of Aberdeen.
The Vocational Aspects of Education
  Triangle. Published three times a year.
  Manuscripts to: B Bailey, School of Post-Compulsory Education and
  Training, University of Greenwich, London.
Westminster Studies in Education
  Carfax. Published annually.
  Manuscripts to: W F Fearon, Westminster College, Oxford.

Annotated Reading List

American Psychological Association (1983) *Publication Manual of the American
  Psychological Association* (3rd edn), Washington, DC: American
  Psychological Association.
  A guide to the style for formal research papers required by a number of
  international journals.
Cave, R and Cave, J (1985) *Writing for Promotion and Profit: A guide to
  educational publishing,* Newmarket: Ron and Joyce Cave Educational
  Consultants.
  A short, rather over-simplified manual that concentrates on facts rather
  than skills and provides some useful tips on getting published. It may help
  you to understand the contract, once you receive it.
Berry, R (1986) *How to Write a Research Paper,* Oxford: Pergamon.
  A short book that covers a number of technical aspects, such as preparing
  a bibliography and dealing with footnotes, that I have not had space to
  cover in this chapter. Worth reading if you are new to publishing and lack
  a source of expert advice.
Open University Press (1993) *An Equal Opportunities Guide to Language and
  Image,* Buckingham: Open University Press.

Many publishers have guides to inclusive language. If yours does not, essential that you are aware of the hidden messages that your use of language may convey. The Open University Press guide is very short (19 pages), simple and user-friendly.
Collected Original Sources in Education, Carfax.
A microfiche journal dealing with original international educational research in full.

The following journals, all from Carfax, provide summaries of many hundred journal articles and/or books published across the world each year. They are a useful means of identifying the most up-to-date research and debate in particular areas of enquiry within education.

Research into Higher Education Abstracts	*Contents Pages in Education*
Educational Technology	*Higher Education Abstracts*
Multicultural Education Abstracts	*Special Educational Needs Abstracts*
Sociology of Education Abstracts	*Technical Education and Training Abstracts.*

References

Ashcroft, K, Bigger, S and Coates, D (1996) *Researching into Equal Opportunities in Colleges and Universities,* London: Kogan Page.

Ashcroft, K and Palacio, D (1996) *Researching into Assessment and Evaluation in Colleges and Universities,* London: Kogan Page.

Bennett, C, Foreman-Peck, L and Higgins, C (1996) *Researching into Teaching Methods in Colleges and Universities,* London: Kogan Page.

Jones, M, Siraj-Blatchford, J and Ashcroft, K (1996) *Researching into Student Support in Colleges and Universities,* London: Kogan Page.

Acknowledgements

I am particularly grateful to John Owens of David Fulton Publishers for much of the background information about the publisher's perspective that is included in this chapter.

I would like to thank Peter Knight of SEDA, Naomi Roth of Cassell Publishers, Oxford University Press, John Skelton of Open University Press, Liz Cartell of Framework Press, Elisabeth Tribe of Hodder and Stoughton Educational, Pat Lomax of Kogan Page, and Jessica Kingsley for their willingness to give up their time to provide me with the information to make this chapter as useful to the reader as possible.

Index